At Issue

Human
Embryo Experimentation

Other Books in the At Issue Series:

At Issue

Human Embryo Experimentation

Christine Watkins, Book Editor

GREENHAVEN PRESS
A part of Gale, Cengage Learning

Detroit • New York • San Francisco • New Haven, Conn • Waterville, Maine • London

GALE
CENGAGE Learning

Christine Nasso, *Publisher*
Elizabeth Des Chenes, *Managing Editor*

© 2011 Greenhaven Press, a part of Gale, Cengage Learning.

Gale and Greenhaven Press are registered trademarks used herein under license.

For more information, contact:
Greenhaven Press
27500 Drake Rd.
Farmington Hills, MI 48331-3535
Or you can visit our Internet site at gale.cengage.com

For product information and technology assistance, contact us at

Gale Customer Support, 1-800-877-4253
For permission to use material from this text or product, submit all requests online at www.cengage.com/permissions

Further permissions questions can be emailed to permissionrequest@cengage.com

Articles in Greenhaven Press anthologies are often edited for length to meet page requirements. In addition, original titles of these works are changed to clearly present the main thesis and to explicitly indicate the author's opinion. Every effort is made to ensure that Greenhaven Press accurately reflects the original intent of the authors. Every effort has been made to trace the owners of copyrighted material.

Cover Image copyright © Images.com/Corbis.

LIBRARY OF CONGRESS CATALOGING-IN-PUBLICATION DATA

Human embryo experimentation / Christine Watkins, book editor.
    p. cm. -- (At issue)
    Includes bibliographical references and index.
    ISBN 978-0-7377-5580-0 (hardcover) -- ISBN ISBN 978-0-7377-5581-7 (pbk.)
    1. Embryonic stem cells--Research. 2. Human embryo--Research. 3. Human experimentation in medicine--Moral and ethical aspects. I. Watkins, Christine, 1951- II. Title. III. Series.
    QH588.S83H832 2011
    616'.02774--dc22
                                                              2011000938

Printed in the United States of America
1 2 3 4 5 6 7 15 14 13 12 11

Contents

Introduction

The assisted reproduction technique of in vitro fertilization—once considered by many to be an abomination of humanity and a moral outrage—has enabled hundreds of thousands of infertile couples to give birth to their own children. In fact, over one million children throughout the world have been born as a result of in vitro fertilization (IVF). An unforeseen consequence, however, is that the IVF process inevitably creates many excess embryos. According to a 2002 Rand Corporation study, approximately 400,000 leftover frozen embryos are stored in liquid nitrogen in clinic freezers throughout the United States, and today the number is probably closer to 500,000. So what should happen to these excess embryos? Should ever-increasing numbers of them be left in a state of suspended animation? Should they be thrown away or thawed and allowed to die off? Or should they be donated to embryonic stem cell research to find cures for diseases? These questions lie at the heart of an extremely contentious and impassioned debate among politicians, research scientists, religious leaders, political action groups, and the general public regarding human embryonic stem cell research.

The central question in the debate is when human life actually begins, and the various answers cause many people to consider issues about life and death, science and religion. As Eve Herold wrote in her 2006 book *Stem Cell Wars: Inside Stories from the Frontlines*:

> While we're making up our minds about this new science, there's another factor to consider that is just as important to most of us as our health: the matter of a good conscience. In spite of how much we could all be affected by the life-saving breakthroughs of stem cell research, the vast majority of us feel that we should only be heir to research that is morally ethical. Who among us would be callous enough to

go through life blithely accepting the idea that his own good health depended on the cruel sacrifice of innocent others.

Most people who repudiate embryonic stem cell research do so because they believe the embryo is a human being— granted, at the very earliest stage, but still a human being. And because the process of harvesting stem cells destroys the embryo at approximately the sixth day of its development, these people view stem cell research to be as morally abhorrent as harvesting organs from a fully-developed human infant. Pope Benedict XVI stated in the *Instruction Dignitas Personae on Certain Bioethical Questions*, published by the Congregation for the Doctrine of the Faith in December 2008, "The obtaining of stem cells from a living human embryo . . . invariably causes the death of the embryo and is consequently gravely illicit. . . . In fact, this research advances through the suppression of human lives that are equal in dignity to the lives of other human individuals." And Fritz J. Baumgartner, a physician with the Harbor-UCLA Medical Center in California, specifically addressed the use of frozen embryos left over from IVF treatments that are "destined to die anyway." He wrote in his April 2009 article "Federal Funding of Human Embryonic Stem Cell Research Revisited: Does the Nobility of Hoped-For Ends Absolve Us?":

> This again leads to the moral analogy posed by the Nuremberg Medical Trials, in which the Nazi defense attorneys used this precise approach to justify medical experimentation on prisoners 'destined to die anyway.' Blanket acceptance of such a philosophy would also justify the ethics of experimenting or organ procurement on prisoners on death-row for the sake of medical utility.

On the other side of the debate are those people in favor of embryonic stem cell research, most of whom believe an embryo should not be considered a human being. These advocates emphasize the important difference between an embryo and a fetus, especially an embryo stored at an IVF clinic.

Because many experts do not consider a fertilized egg to be an actual embryo until it attaches to the wall of a woman's uterus, the embryos stored in test tubes are actually "pre-embryos." There are no body parts because there is no body, no nerve cells to feel pain, no brain, no consciousness, and no self-awareness. A fetus, however, has already established a pregnancy by attaching to a woman's body and is at a much later stage of development, usually two months after conception. As pro-life Republican and California state representative Dana Rohrabacher told Liza Mundy in an interview for her article "Souls on Ice: America's Embryo Glut and the Wasted Promise of Stem Cell Research" featured in the July/August 2006 issue of *Mother Jones*, "I have done a lot of soul-searching but also a lot of rethinking about reality. . . . I don't think that the potential for human life exists in a human embryo until it's implanted in a human body. . . . Left alone, they will not become a human being."

In fact, many religious Americans and organizations—including the United Methodist Church, the United Church of Christ, the Unitarian Universalist Association, and the Episcopal Church—share Rohrabacher's view and support research using embryos that would otherwise be discarded. They regard curing the sick to be a more ethical and beneficial disposition for leftover IVF embryos than existing in a frozen state.

The controversy over the personhood and proper dispensation of unimplanted embryos shows no sign of diminishing, and the likelihood of a consensus anytime soon appears improbable. Again from Eve Harold's book *Stem Cell Wars: Inside Stories from the Frontlines*, "The future of embryonic stem cell research depends, quite simply, on whether we believe that a person is destroyed in the process. And the answer to that question cannot be provided by science—it is inevitably a matter of belief." The viewpoints in *At Issue: Human Embryo Experimentation* reflect other perspectives on this passionately debated topic.

1

Human Embryonic Research Benefits Society

Coalition for the Advancement of Medical Research (CAMR)

The Coalition for the Advancement of Medical Research (CAMR) is comprised of more than 100 nationally recognized patient organizations, universities, scientific societies, and foundations. CAMR's advocacy and education outreach focuses on developing better treatment and cures for individuals with life-threatening illnesses and disorders.

The study of human embryonic stem cells (hESC) is showing more progress than ever before in devising cures for many debilitating diseases. Researchers have proven that stem cells from embryos can be made into any kind of cell in the body; experimenting with and studying the reactions of these cells will result in the development of safer and more effective drugs for the treatment and cure of such diseases as cancer, diabetes, and Lou Gehrig's disease. Access to human embryonic stem cells is crucial for the progress and benefit to society to continue.

Human embryonic stem cell (hESC) research has reached a 10-year milestone. In 1998, James Thomson [director of regenerative biology at the University of Wisconsin School of Medicine and Public Health] and John Gearhart [director of the Institute for Regenerative Medicine, University of Pennsylvania] separately announced they had successfully grown the first human pluripotent stem cell lines in culture, cells that

Excerpt from "A Catalyst for Cures: Embryonic Cell Research," Coalition for the Advancement of Medical Research, January 12, 2009, pp. 4–10. Reproduced by permission of Coalition for the Advancement of Medical Research.

can self-renew and give rise to various cell types in the body. Despite limited funding, scientists have made great strides in using these primary cells to understand what goes wrong in disease and begin to devise promising new therapies for devastating conditions, such as heart disease, spinal cord injury, and diabetes. Conversations with some of the nation's top stem cell researchers—in academia and industry—make clear that, with removal of limits on federal funding, hESC research will fulfill its promise in broader ways than, originally anticipated.

It is time for the government to become a full scientific partner in supporting the broad range of stem cell research so that the greatest public benefit can be achieved on the shoulders of the last 10 years' accomplishments.

Stem Cell Research Is More Promising than Ever

In 1998, researchers imagined that hES cells could be made into any kind of cell in the body. Ten years ago, this was a hope. Today it is fact. Researchers have shown that stem cells from embryos have the ability to become many of the roughly 210 cell types in the human body. They have coaxed hES cells to form heart cells, dopamine-producing brain cells, motor neurons, bladder tissue, kidney tissue, and others.

Two out of three major, early goals for hES cells have been met:

1. hES cells would be a vehicle for learning about tissue development and about the relationship of tissues and genes. They would lead to the discovery of the genes involved in self-renewal. Those promises have been realized.

2. hES cells would offer a path to new treatments. Now that Scientists know how to make heart muscle and dopamine-producing cells, for example, the goals of cell

therapies have moved from the theoretical to the concrete, hESC-derived cells are beginning to be used for early toxicity screening and new drug discovery, as well.

3. There would be widespread use and testing of these cells. Restrictive federal policies severely diminished that expectation.

"Everything we expected hES cells to do, they are doing," says James Thomson, University of Wisconsin. "They've proven themselves."

"In the next decade, most advances will come from drugs that affect progression of disease. And we'll get there by using hES cells as test beds for new therapeutics," says Doug Melton, Harvard Stem Cell Institute.

---

hES cells are an unbeatable research tool to understand the body and what goes wrong in disease.

After 10 years of experience with hES cells, scientists know what needs to be done to make ES-based cells useful for patients—and the opportunities go far beyond cell transplantation.

The scientific community is asking questions it would not have asked if it didn't have access to hES cells. And hES cell studies led to the unexpected development of induced pluripotent stem (iPS) cells, adult cells that are reprogrammed to an embryonic stem cell-like state by being forced to express factors important for maintaining pluripotency. Now we even have proof that you can take a fully mature cell and put genes into it and drive it in a different direction. Pancreatic exocrine cells, for example, can be transformed to pancreatic beta cells, the cells that are destroyed in type 1 diabetes. All of these advances are a result of hES cell research.

The big revolution in the next 10 years will focus on the ability to make the cell types that get sick and use them for drug discovery, removing the study of disease from people to a Petri dish. This has never been possible before—and its one of the main reasons the drug pipeline has not been flowing with new, effective drugs. . . .

Human Embryonic Stem Cells Have a Crucial Role

hES cells are an unbeatable research tool to understand the body and what goes wrong in disease. Just like telescopes opened new vistas to distant galaxies, hES cells offer unprecedented access to the human body. Scientists are using hES cells to grow limitless quantities of various tissues, such as heart muscle cells. It will be a vast improvement over today's studies of the physiology of the human heart, which rely on limited biopsy samples from sick hearts.

Some opposed to hESC research have argued that we don't need hES cells anymore, now that iPS cells have been developed. But if we have learned anything in the history of stem cell research, it is that we have not been very good at predicting which cells are most useful for which applications. To devise new therapies, research must continue with all types of stem cells. If we allow research on hES cells to wither, who knows how many other breakthroughs, like adult cell reprogramming, will go undiscovered. Although iPS cells show great promise, preliminary studies indicate they are not identical to hES cells and may not be as useful for some applications. And there appears to be significant variation between iPS cell lines, probably more so than between human ES cell lines. Further studies are necessary. In terms of safety, iPS cells are much further from the clinic than are ES cells. At present, they are made with genes and viruses that can cause cancer.

"We are doing very careful comparisons of how well iPS cells and hES cells make motor neurons, and how functional those cells truly are," says Kevin Eggan, Harvard University. "NIH [National Institutes of Health] should be funding both activities."

Every study of iPS cells requires hES cells for controls and comparisons. These comparisons are crucial for moving the iPS field forward. Researchers must test the safety and efficacy of iPS cells against hES cells. Continued research on hES cells and others may reveal other ways to accomplish regenerative medicine. But we are not there yet.

Finally, and importantly, federal restrictions on hES cell lines are a social justice issue. The federal lines do not represent the diversity in our society. If hES cells have the potential to change the future of medicine, our federal government has imposed restrictions that might lead to minorities being left out of that future. The same federal government that insists on enrolling diverse patients in any clinical trial to ensure that new medicines work in everyone, insists that researchers do all work on hES cells that are from a small number of sources.

All Research Avenues Should Be Utilized

Many scientists have been studying adult stem cells and learning more about their utility and their limitations. So far, adult stem cells have only successfully been used in a very narrow area: blood system reconstitution, including bone marrow transplant, umbilical cord transplant, and peripheral blood transplant.

"If you're a botanist, you don't study one type of tree to learn everything about trees," says Ole Isacson, [professor of neurology at] Harvard Medical School.

This is a war against disease and it needs to be fought with all weapons.

In 2006, [Shinya] Yamanaka [Japanese physician and stem cell researcher] first reported he had turned mouse adult skin cells into stem cells. Then late in 2007, Yamanaka, Thomson, and [George] Daley [associate professor of biological chemistry and molecular pharmacology at Harvard Medical School] each reported that they had successfully turned human adult skin cells into stem cells. The development of these iPS cells was unexpected. The prevailing wisdom was that, once a cell had become differentiated or specialized, it could not be turned back by any method other than nuclear transfer. But that's just what iPS does. iPS cells are a victory for ES cells. They demonstrate the power of stem cell science to lead to unexpected and field-changing breakthroughs.

Recall the recombinant DNA [a form of artificial DNA] debates of the mid 1970s. Some thought recombinant DNA technology was so dangerous it should be banned outright. But reason prevailed, and science went forward, and recombinant DNA has dramatically changed human medicine. For example, insulin was cloned using recombinant DNA technology. If decision-makers had sided with fear, and stopped this research, millions of people who are thriving on recombinant insulin would have died. . . .

The bottom line is, all areas of stem cell research should remain open. "It's not our job to guess right now what we will need in the future and how," says Sean Morrison, [professor of cell and development biology at the] University of Michigan. "This is a war against disease and it needs to be fought with all weapons." . . .

"Embryonic research is not the unregulated 'wild west' of science," says Sean Morrison.

Guidelines for the ethical oversight and ongoing monitoring of stem cell research have been developed by the National Academies and the International Society for Stem Cell Research. Many institutions have already adopted these guidelines, which require each institution conducting stem cell research to have a protocol-by-protocol ethical review of the work by a committee of ethicists, scientists, legal experts, and community members. These so-called ESCRO (Embryonic

Stem Cell Research Oversight) committees are focused specifically on the ethical implications of using human embryonic stem cell lines in scientific research. Additional supervision is afforded by other pre-existing federally mandated oversight committees, such as institutional review boards in the case of human subjects research, animal care committees, and committees on biological safety. If federal policies change, there is already a framework in place to devise federal guidelines on the use of these materials. . . .

Public opinion strongly favors embryonic stem cell research. Nearly three-quarters (73%) of Americans believe that President-elect [Barack] Obama should keep his pledge to lift existing federal restrictions on embryonic stem cell research, according to a national poll conducted for CAMR in January 2009 by Opinion Research Corporation. November's [2008] U.S. election also showed the public's support. In Michigan, voters decided to let scientists derive new human embryonic stem cell lines from embryos donated by couples getting fertility treatments. Michigan had one of the country's most restrictive laws on embryonic stem cell research and the ballot proposal to loosen restrictions succeeded despite an extremely well-funded opposition campaign. A Colorado measure that would define a fertilized egg as a human being was also defeated.

Progress on Several Disease Fronts Is Foreseeable

"It's like discovering nuclear power . . . and now we have to figure out how to use it," says Ole Isacson. His group discovered they could make dopamine-producing cells from hES cells in 2002. But it took much more work to learn how to modify the factors that control the process, and how to do it consistently and with high efficiency. Research takes time. A few examples from history:

- The poliovirus was first isolated in 1909. It took 45 years to get to the Salk vaccine.

- HIV was first isolated in 1983. Bringing all the power of modern virology—and billions of dollars to bear— hundreds of scientists are still working on combating this virus.

- The first attempt at bone marrow transplantation be- tween an unrelated donor and recipient was in 1955 by E. Donnall Thomas—after many years of research. All six patients died. He went back to the lab to figure out why. The first successful transplant of these adult stem cells occurred in 1969—14 years later. It took years more of clinical testing to get it right, and bone mar- row transplantation only became a common procedure in the 1980s. If opponents, after 10 years of study of these adult stem cells, had said "there've been no cures, let's stop," then adult cell transplantation would not exist and countless lives would not have been saved.

Scientists need the time and support to overcome safety concerns for using ES cells in patients. There won't be prod- ucts for patients unless scientists can devise ways to eliminate risk. Parkinson's researcher Ole Isacson is sorting stem-cell de- rived neural cells to remove those that have tumor-cause po- tential. This isn't headline-grabbing, but it's critical science. Researchers need to explore what happens to cells once they are transplanted, determine the immune system's reaction to the cells, and see if there are cancer risks. Are the cells com- patible with any drugs the patient might be taking for their disease or other conditions? Can the cells tolerate those drugs?

Cancer chemotherapy: Researchers are studying ES cells, close cousins to cancer cells, to learn how cancer cells repli- cate. ES cells may be used as a drug target for cancer cells. They may also be used to personalize cancer therapies. Before a cancer patient takes a chemotherapy regimen that is extremely toxic, doctors could take a skin cell from the patient, and through the iPS process, create liver cells and heart cells. The chemotherapy could be tested first on those patient's "own" cells. A new drug regimen would only be given to the patient after it is clear that the drugs will kill the cancer, not the patient.

Diabetes: "Everything we've learned says we will get there. If there are seven steps to turn an ES cell into a pancreatic beta cell, we've solved two of the steps," says Doug Melton. "We will get there, but it may be a year or a decade." Geron [biotechnology company] and Novocell [stem cell engineering company] are developing cell therapy. Geron has shown it can put hES cell-derived therapy in mice and improve function and extend life.

Spinal cord injury: Spinal cord cell types were the first high purity, commercially scalable cells derived from hES cells. Hans Keirstead's [associate professor of anatomy and neurobiology] group at UC Irvine has been working with Geron to address the four major challenges in treatment development: manufacturing the product so it is suitable for human use, studies to show the treatment works in animals, and is safe in animals, and development of a clinical plan to apply the treatment to humans.

Parkinson's disease: Several groups have made dopamine-producing nerve cells from hES cells and iPS cells. They have shown they work in animal models. Scientists are also using the nerve cells to study the mechanisms of the disease in hopes of devising treatments that will stop its progression.

Age-related macular degeneration: hES cells converted into the special cells that line the base of the retina have rescued vision in rats with a form of this blinding disease.

Amyotrophic lateral sclerosis (ALS) or Lou Gehrig's disease: Ordinary skin cells taken from patients with ALS were transformed into iPS cells and then motor neurons, the cells that waste away and die in ALS. Now the researchers can make unlimited supplies of these cells to uncover the mechanisms behind this disease and screen for drugs that can prolong life.

Heart disease: Scientists have made cardiac cells from hES cells that beat in a dish. Geron has a very large program in this area. It will likely be their second clinical application. They've seen functional improvements in animal models. A group in Wisconsin is building toxicology screens using cardiomyocytes, [cells that comprise cardiac muscle] since heart toxicity is the most common drug toxicity today, along with liver toxicity. This group is testing drugs that have already failed clinical testing on cardiomyocytes from hESCs as early predictors of drug failure. They're not putting cells into patients, but it will have a huge impact on patients.

The Benefit from Embryonic Stem Cell Therapy Is Exaggerated

Gene Tarne and David Prentice

Gene Tarne is the communications director of Do No Harm: The Coalition of Americans for Research Ethics, an organization dedicated to the promotion of scientific research and health care that does no harm to human life. David Prentice is a professor and expert on stem cell research and a senior fellow for life sciences at the Family Research Council, a conservative Christian organization that promotes the interest of the traditional family.

Scientists involved with human embryonic stem cell research (hESCR), eager for federal funding, often manipulate data and overstate the potential of embryonic stem cells in order to sway public and political opinion in their favor. Their tactics have been successful in that some state senators and representatives, patient advocacy groups, and even celebrities have made extravagant claims that hESCR will ultimately cure and eliminate such diseases as Alzheimer's, Parkinson's, and diabetes, repair spinal cord injuries, and save millions of lives. The reality is that little scientific evidence supports these assertions. In fact, research using adult stem cells has proven more effective in treating diseases without provoking the moral and ethical objections associated with the use of human embryos.

Gene Tarne and David Prentice, "Playing Politics with Stem Cells," *American Thinker*, August 8, 2010. Reproduced by permission of *American Thinker*.

When scientists play politics with science, society and science both suffer, sometimes with life-threatening implications. One recent example is Climategate, with revelations that leading global warming researchers played with the data, concealed and tried to suppress data that challenged their assertions, and attempted to game the peer review system. And as a result of scientists caught playing politics with science, claims of man-made global warming have been met with growing skepticism.

But a similar scenario has played out regarding human embryonic stem cell research (hESCR). With the introduction of legislation to codify the [Barack] Obama administration's rules expanding the federal role in funding hESCR, it's time that the extravagant claims for such research suffer the same fate.

Mixing Scientific Evidence with Politics

Like Climategate, the public policy debate over hESCR has shown that scientists are not always disinterested parties. Rather, scientists can be every bit as political and partisan as the politicians, selectively using scientific "evidence" to justify their ideological viewpoint.

> *The scientific facts regarding hESCR are remarkably flimsy and incapable of supporting the extravagant claims for such research.*

The patterns of behavior promoting public funding of hESCR have been strikingly similar to Climategate: selective use of data, manipulation of the peer review process, demonizing colleagues who question the prevailing orthodoxies, and appeals to a bogus scientific "consensus," among others. Those who question this supposed "consensus" have been dismissed as scientifically ignorant and accused of playing politics with science.

Indeed, President [George W.] Bush's policy on hESCR was a prime example of what opponents dubbed the "war on science." Their narrative, dutifully echoed by the mainstream media, was that limiting federal funding of hESCR showed that Bush was either ignorant or contemptuous of science, willing to play politics to appease his pro-life base.

In contrast, President Obama characterized his executive order lifting the Bush-era restrictions as "ensuring that scientific data is never distorted or concealed to serve a political agenda, and that we make scientific decisions based on facts, not ideology."

His remarks were risible. The scientific facts regarding hESCR are remarkably flimsy and incapable of supporting the extravagant claims for such research. Such claims advance a political agenda—legitimizing and guaranteeing federal funding for ethically contentious research. For the same political reasons, the increasingly strong evidence of actual therapeutic benefits to patients from ethically non-contentious adult stem cell research was distorted or concealed.

Senator Arlen Specter [Pennsylvania] declared that hESCR "could result in a veritable fountain of youth by replacing diseased or damaged cells." Sen. Tom Harkin [Iowa] said in 2005 that apart from Hurricane Katrina relief, the most urgent issue facing the nation was lifting the Bush restrictions on hESCR because "people are dying from diseases and medical conditions that might be cured through embryonic stem-cell research. . . . [E]very day of delay by the Senate has life-and-death consequences." Nancy Pelosi [speaker of the U.S. House of Representatives] waxed theological, saying "Scientists have been given an almost biblical power to cure through advances in embryonic stem cell research".

The "Law of Exaggerated Expectations"

Many patient advocacy groups—and celebrities associated with them—also were not shy in hyping hESCR. The Alliance for Aging Research said that it allows us to "imagine a world without debilitating costly diseases such as Parkinson's, heart disease and diabetes." [Actor] Michael J. Fox flatly stated that hESCR has the "potential to eliminate diseases, literally save millions of lives", while Christopher Reeve [deceased actor] told a Senate committee, "For the true biological miracles that researchers have only begun to foresee, medical science must turn to undifferentiated [embryonic] stem cells."

Scientists themselves—eager for federal research dollars but determined that no one outside the "research community" should tell them what they could or could not do—also joined in.

The five- to ten-year predictions were apparently designed to mislead people into thinking treatments were imminent.

Then-NIH [National Institutes of Health] director Harold Varmus testified that "within the course of the next decade or two ... many diseases would be at least treated, if not entirely cured" by embryonic stem cells. Michael West, president and CEO of Advanced Cell Technologies, declared embryonic stem cells among the gifts "that mankind occasionally is given ... that can greatly advance the human condition." Dr. Bert Vogelstein of Johns Hopkins University testified that embryonic stem cells would prove beneficial "for any of these diseases: Alzheimer's disease, Parkinson's disease, a variety of spinal cord injuries, certain types of diabetes, many others ... The only hope on the horizon is through transplantation of these [embryonic] stem cells."

By the rhetorical standards set by hESCR proponents, Varmus' prediction that many diseases would be treated "within the next decade or two" was conservative. More often, proponents would offer five to ten years. Jose Cibelli, a leading proponent of hESCR, admitted that such pronouncements were essentially meaningless. Asked when therapies using hESCs would be ready, Cibelli told the Baltimore Sun, "My answer is five years. It's the same thing as saying I have no idea."

Five and even ten years have come and gone, and there are no treatments or cures using hESCs. One clinical trial approved by the FDA [U.S. Food and Drug Administration] in 2009, then put on safety hold, was reapproved in July 2010, but as yet, not a single patient has even been injected with hESC. The five- to ten-year predictions were apparently designed to mislead people into thinking treatments were imminent, and to realize them, all Congress needed to do was expand federal hESCR funding.

In 1992, journalist Gregg Easterbrook, writing on the global warming debate, coined what he called the "Law of Doomsaying": "Predict dreadful events whose arrival impends no sooner than 5 years hence, no later than 10"—i.e., soon enough to scare people into action, but far enough away that they will not recall if your predictions prove wrong. In the hESCR debate, let's call it the "Law of Exaggerated Expectations": Predict wildly optimistic outcomes for cures no later than ten years hence, but no sooner than five years away—a seemingly reasonable time to raise expectations and support for the research, but far enough off that people will forget if it is wrong.

Even the respected *New England Journal of Medicine* [NEJM] jumped on the bandwagon, announcing its willingness to distort the peer review process to promote embryonic stem cell research. In July 2003, the NEJM announced it would give preferential treatment to publishing papers that shed a favorable light on hESCR. And it did so for explicitly political purposes—to "boost the controversial field's standing among politicians and the public."

It certainly needed a boost—very little scientific evidence supports hESCR. Nonetheless, the "scientific community" insisted there was a "consensus" that embryonic stem cells had the greatest potential to cure any number of diseases, period. This bogus "scientific consensus" soon became the new orthodoxy, and there was to be no dissent.

Embryonic stem cells have achieved nothing regarding MS even in animal models.

In April 2007, *Nature Neuroscience* set its sights on Maureen Condic, professor of Neurobiology and Anatomy at the University of Utah. In an editorial, the journal attacked her for being "anti-scientific" and "polemical" and engaging in "disingenuous distortions of scientific arguments." Her crime? In the pages of *First Things* (the editorial attack pointedly described it as a "conservative Roman Catholic magazine"), Prof. Condic, relying on the peer-reviewed, published literature, challenged the prevailing orthodoxy, throwing much-needed cold water on the extravagant hESCR claims, going so far as to suggest that adult stem cells may well prove to be more efficacious in actually helping patients!

In 2002, Roger Pielke, Director of the Center for Science and Technology Policy Research at the University of Colorado, noted in the journal *Nature* the trend to politicize science: "As political battles are waged through 'science', many scientists are willing to adopt tactics of demagoguery and character assassination as well as, or even instead of, reasoned argument ... science is increasingly the battlefield on which political advocates, not to mention lawyers and those with commercial interests, manipulate 'facts' to support their positions."

Disparaging the Potential of Adult Stem Cells

Or ignore facts altogether. In 2007, Sen. Tom Harkin waved away evidence for adult stem cells, saying, "Scientists have known about adult stem cells for forty years, and they still haven't provided the answer for juvenile diabetes." He said this on the very day that the *Journal of the American Medical Association* (JAMA) published clinical trial results using adult stem cells in a treatment that reversed juvenile diabetes in patients.

In a May 2008 House committee hearing, Weyman Johnson, board chair of the National Multiple Sclerosis Society and an MS sufferer himself, testified that "embryonic stem cell research holds unique promise to repair nerve cells to slow the progression of MS and to find a cure." Yet in February 2008, JAMA published data showing benefits of adult stem cells for patients with various auto-immune diseases, including MS. Embryonic stem cells have achieved nothing regarding MS even in animal models.

At that same hearing, Rep. Diana DeGette [Colorado] commented that "I know that these wonderful patients who are here today who have been cured by adult stem cells, mostly for blood-related diseases, would never say that somebody with diabetes or somebody with Parkinson's or somebody with nerve damage or somebody with macular degeneration—all diseases for which embryonic stem cell research has shown promise and adult stem cells have shown no clinical promise—no one would say those people should not be cured . . ."

She was zero for four. Rep. DeGette seemed embarrassingly unaware of the year-old JAMA study showing adult stem cells' efficacy for juvenile diabetes patients—and Rep. DeGette is co-chair of the Congressional Diabetes Caucus.

Parkinson's? In 2004, both Dr. Michel Levesque and Dennis Turner, a Parkinson's patient Levesque treated with Turner's own adult stem cells, testified regarding the positive results of the treatment. Leveque subsequently published his findings in the peer-reviewed *Bentham Open Stem Cell Journal*.

Nerve damage? Published studies using adult stem cells to treat spinal cord injuries include a 2006 report by Portugal's Dr. Carlos Lima in collaboration with Dr. Jean Peduzzi-Nelson of Wayne State University. They published a second report in 2009 using adult stem cells to treat more spinal cord injured patients.

Macular degeneration? Far from showing "no clinical promise," University of Louisville researchers have announced plans for a human trial of adult stem cells for macular degeneration. Rep. DeGette also seemed completely oblivious to the fact that the patient who testified was treated with his own adult stem cells for heart damage, not a "blood-related disease."

This was a remarkable display of ignorance by one of the leading proponents of hESCR. But DeGette went even farther in dismissing evidence inconvenient to her political agenda. "It makes me particularly angry when people try to claim that adult stem cells can substitute for cures for diseases for which adult stem cells have shown no clinical promise whatsoever[.]"

Her remark showed the flip-side of hyping hESCR to advance a political agenda—demonize and dismiss those who disagree.

Given the ethical problems associated with hESCR, it should not even be undertaken if viable alternatives exist.

At one Senate hearing, Dr. Jean Peduzzi-Nelson outlined her research showing positive adult stem cell treatment for spinal cord injury. Yet Sen. Frank Lautenberg's first question for her was "Are you a member of a pro-life group?"—repeating it with an even more McCarthyesque tinge: "Are you now a member of a pro-life group in any way?" Simply identifying someone as pro-life was apparently sufficient reason to dismiss his or her scientific facts.

The mainstream media joined in: the *Washington Post's* Rick Weiss, in a "news" report, identified opponents of embryo cloning as "religious conservatives" and not so subtly compared them to the Taliban.

When President [William Jefferson] Clinton's National Bioethics Advisory Committee (NBAC) recommended federal funding for hESCR, it did so conditionally: "In our judgment, the derivation of stem cells from embryos remaining following infertility treatments is justifiable only if no less morally problematic alternatives are available for advancing the research ... The claim that there are alternatives to using stem cells derived from embryos is not, at the present time, supported scientifically. *We recognize, however, that this is a matter that must be revisited continually as science advances*" (emphasis added).

In other words, they recognized that given the ethical problems associated with hESCR, it should not even be undertaken if viable alternatives exist.

A "Sense of Propriety"

But the insistence on continuing hESCR in the name of cures raises the question as to whether the NBAC was simply being disingenuous when it said hESCR should be pursued only if no alternatives are available. It now seems nothing more than a clever political ploy, designed to allay concerns over the ethically contentious nature of hESCR. Lip service to "advances of science" showing the efficacy of alternatives would not derail the political drive for federal funding of hESCR.

The most ironic—and most troubling—aspect to the stem cell debate is that all the talk about "playing politics" with science obscured the fact that in an open society, there is and must be a role for politics in determining the parameters within which science will be conducted. By itself, science is not competent to set these parameters. Science is a method to obtain knowledge; it can determine that one way may be more effective or more efficient than another. But efficient does not always mean morally acceptable.

In congressional testimony, Dr. Stuart Newman, a professor at New York Medical College, offered a hypothetical. Researchers have agreed among themselves that fourteen days is the outer limit to destroy embryos to obtain their stem cells. But, Newman wondered, why stop there? After all, more valuable cells could be obtained from cloned embryos allowed to develop to eight to nine weeks. "Right now, it would be a hot potato, but once we have . . . gotten used to the idea . . . And once stem cell harvesting from two-month clonal embryos is in place, who could resist the pleas to extend the time frame . . .? I emphasize that all of this makes perfectly good scientific and medical sense. The only thing that stands in the way is the sense of propriety concerning the uses to which developing human embryos and fetuses may be put."

Our "sense of propriety" must of necessity be based on something other than science. We (currently at least) reject such research not because it is scientifically unsound, but because we sense it is morally and ethically beyond the pale. Refusing to permit research that may be the most efficient from a scientific perspective because of ethical concerns may make the research more costly and time-consuming to pursue—but that cost is the price we pay to keep our humanity.

That is why in an open society, determining public policy on science requires hearing from many voices, voices from outside the scientific community such as ethicists, religious leaders, economists, philosophers, and others, in addition to members of the scientific community. The perspectives they bring should not and must not be dismissed as ideological, sectarian, or narrow-minded. Just as war is too important to leave to the generals, setting public policy on science is too important to leave to the scientists.

By the same token, when actual scientific evidence is dismissed because it is inconvenient to political goals, then all that's left is the politics. And once that happens, all that's left is to use the issue to score political points off your opponents.

By the time President Obama signed his executive order vastly expanding the role of the federal government in hESCR, the actual science of stem cell research advances to help patients had long ago left the building. Should Rep. DeGette succeed in passing her legislation, it will not protect the president's executive order from politics. It will, though, protect it from science.

3

An Embryo Should Be Considered a Human Being

Robert P. George and Christopher Tollefsen

*Robert P. George, a member of the President's Council on Bio-
ethics, is a professor of jurisprudence and director of the James
Madison Program in American Ideals and Institutions at Prince-
ton University. He is the author of* Making Men Moral *and* In
Defense of Natural Law. *Christopher Tollefsen is an associate
professor in the philosophy department at the University of
South Carolina and is the author of* Biomedical Research and
Beyond.

*Scientists in many countries, including the United States, have
become so excited by and intrigued with creating medical treatments and cures derived from human embryonic stem cells that
they are overlooking an important ethical question: is it morally
permissible to deliberately destroy human embryos for therapeutic purposes? After all, a human embryo is not just a tiny part of
an organism, nor is it just a clump of cells. It is, in fact, a human being at its very early stage of development. Every person
in this world begins as an embryo; to kill an embryo is to kill
that person. Morality and the sanctity of all human life must be
regarded as higher in value than biomedical research.*

On January 16, 2007, a remarkable journey came to an
end in Covington, Louisiana. Sixteen months earlier,
Noah Benton Markham's life had been jeopardized by the

winds and rain of Hurricane Katrina. Trapped in a flooded hospital in New Orleans, Noah depended upon the timely work of seven Illinois Conservation Police officers, and three Louisiana State officers who used flat-bottomed boats to rescue Noah and take him to safety.

The Rescue of Noah

Although many New Orleans residents tragically lost their lives in Katrina and its aftermath, Noah's story of rescue is, nevertheless, one of many inspirational tales of heroism from that national disaster. What, then, makes it unique? And why did the story of his rescue end sixteen months *after* the events of September 2006? The answer is that Noah has the distinction of being one of the youngest residents of New Orleans to be saved from Katrina: when the Illinois and Louisiana police officers entered the hospital where Noah was trapped, he was an embryo, a human being in the very earliest stages of development, frozen with fourteen hundred embryos in canisters of liquid nitrogen.

> *A human embryo is a whole living member of the species Homo sapiens in the earliest stage of his or her natural development.*

Noah's story had a happy ending: Noah's parents were overjoyed those sixteen months later when Noah emerged, via cesarean section, into the light of the wide world. His parents named him in acknowledgment of a resourceful survivor of an earlier flood. His grandmother immediately started phoning relatives with the news: "It's a boy!" But if those officers had never made it to Noah's hospital, or if they had abandoned those canisters of liquid nitrogen, there can be little doubt that the toll of Katrina would have been fourteen hundred human beings higher than it already was, and Noah, sadly, would have perished before having the opportunity to meet his loving family.

Let us repeat it: *Noah* would have perished. For it was Noah who was frozen in one of those canisters; Noah who was brought from New Orleans by boat; Noah who was subsequently implanted into his mother's womb; and Noah who was born on January 16, 2007.

Noah started this remarkable journey as an embryo, or blastocyst—a name for a very early stage of development in a human being's life. Noah continued that journey after implantation into his mother's womb, growing into a fetus and finally an infant. And he will continue, we are confident, to grow into an adolescent and a teenager as he continues along the path to adulthood.

Noah's progress in these respects is little different from that of any other member of the human race, save for the exertions necessary to save him at the very earliest stage of his life. But in later years, if Noah were to look back to that troubled time in New Orleans and ask himself whether *he* was rescued that day, whether it was *his life* that was saved, we believe that there is only one answer he could reasonably give himself: "Of course!"

Some Moral Questions

This answer to Noah's question is a mere two words long, yet it contains the key to one of the most morally and politically troubled issues of our day. Is it morally permissible to produce and experiment upon human embryos? Is it morally permissible to destroy human embryos to obtain stem cells for therapeutic purposes? Is it morally permissible to treat human embryos as disposable research material that may be used and destroyed to benefit others? All such questions have the seeds of their answer in these two words. For what Noah would be saying in these two words—and his answer is confirmed by all the best science—that *human embryos are, from the very beginning, human beings, sharing an identity with, though younger than, the older, human beings they will grow up to become.*

Human embryos are not, that is to say, some other type of animal organism, like a dog or cat. Neither are they a part of an organism, like a heart, a kidney, or a skin cell. Nor again are they a disorganized aggregate, a mere clump of cells awaiting some magical transformation. Rather, a human embryo is a whole living member of the species Homo sapiens in the earliest stage of his or her natural development. Unless severely damaged, or denied or deprived of a suitable environment, a human being in the embryonic stage will, by directing its own integral organic functioning, develop himself or herself to the next more mature developmental stage, i.e., the fetal stage. The embryonic, fetal, child, and adolescent stages are stages in the development of a determinate and enduring entity—a human being—who comes into existence as a single-celled organism (the zygote) and develops, if all goes well, into adulthood many years later.

But does this mean that the human embryo is a human person worthy of full moral respect? Must the early embryo never be used as a mere means for the benefit of others simply because it is a human being? The answer that this book proposes and defends with philosophical arguments . . . is "Yes."

This "yes" has many implications, for human life in its earliest stages and most dependent conditions is under threat today as in no other era. The United States, as well as many of the countries of Europe and the developed countries of Asia, are about to move beyond the past thirty years' experience of largely unrestricted abortion to a whole new regime of human embryo mass production and experimentation. This new regime requires new rationalizations. Whereas, in the past, the humanity of the fetus, or its moral worth, were ignored or denied in favor of an alleged "right to privacy," or considerations of the personal tragedies of women experiencing unwanted pregnancies, what is now proposed is something quite different.

The production of human embryos, and their destruction in biomedical research, will take place in public labs by teams of scientists. If those scientists and their many supporters have their way, their work will be funded, as it is or soon will be in California, New Jersey, and elsewhere, by the state or by the nation, and in either case by taxpayers' money. And if that work bears fruit, then the consequences of this research will be felt throughout the world of medicine and the pharmaceutical industry. It will be virtually impossible for those with grave moral objections to such experimentation to remain free from entanglement in it: their money will pay for labs in their universities, and their doctors will routinely use the results of embryo-destructive research.

The point of the controversy is the ethics of deliberately destroying human embryos for the purpose of producing stem cells.

Clarifying the Moral Issue

For example, in 2004, a ballot initiative known as Proposition 71 was passed in California. This referendum was supported by Arnold Schwarzenegger, the Republican governor of the state. Its backers contributed a tremendous amount of money, and much propaganda, to ensure its passage. The measure promises that up to $3.1 billion will be spent on embryo-destructive research over the next ten years. Even supporters of the research have pointed out that Proposition 71 threatens to bring about a largely unregulated industry that will inevitably line the pockets of a relative few. But such objections, important as they are, ignore what this industry is centrally about: the production and destruction of human beings in the earliest stage of development. This basic truth is lost amidst discussion of "therapeutic cloning" or "Somatic Cell Nuclear Transfer (SCNT)," euphemisms and technicalities designed to obscure rather than clarify. And amidst the promises of boundless health benefits from this research, it can become tempting to lose sight of all that is really at stake. But consider the following analogy.

Suppose that a movement arose to obtain transplantable organs by killing mentally retarded infants. Would the controversy that would inevitably erupt over this be best characterized as a debate about organ transplantation? Would anyone accept as a legitimate description the phrase *therapeutic organ harvesting?* Surely not: the dispute would best be characterized—and in any decent society it would be characterized—as a debate about the ethics of killing retarded children in order to obtain their organs. (Indeed, in a truly decent society, the question would not arise at all!)

Nor would the public, we submit, accept arguments for the practice that turned on considerations about how many gravely ill nonretarded people could be saved by extracting a heart, two kidneys, a liver, etc., from each retarded child. For the threshold question would be whether it is unjust to relegate a certain class of human beings—the retarded—to the status of objects that can be killed and dissected to benefit others. Similarly, there would be something almost obscene in worrying about underregulation of these procedures.

By the same token, we should not be speaking, as in California, in terms of a debate about embryonic stem cell research; nor is the main moral issue that of adequate governmental oversight. No one would object to the use of embryonic stem cells in biomedical research or therapy if they could be derived without killing or in any way wronging the embryos. Nor would anyone object to using such cells if they could be obtained using embryos lost in spontaneous abortions. The point of the controversy is the ethics of deliberately destroying human embryos for the purpose of producing stem cells. The threshold question is whether it is unjust to kill members of a certain class of human beings—those in the embryonic stage of development—to benefit others. Thus we return to the significance of the story of Noah and the flood. . . .

The Sanctity of All Human Life

We live in a difficult age. Convictions once widely shared about the value of unborn human life have been eroded over the past forty years, especially following the Supreme Court's decision in *Roe v. Wade* [the 1973 decision that struck down many laws restricting abortion]. Moreover, intense excitement about the possibility of new knowledge and better health creates incentives that make it difficult to think clearly about our obligations to others, especially when those others are very small, utterly defenseless, and do not look or seem "like us." Competition between nations for scientific prestige and slogans about the march of progress make it seem all but inevitable that embryo-destructive science *will* go forward, without the benefit of sustained moral reflection regarding its ends or its means.

But people who care about justice and human rights should stand fast in the defense of all innocent human life. We hope that the moral reflection we invite people into by presenting our arguments in this book will help them to do just that.

4

An Embryo Should Not Be Considered a Human Being

Ronald A. Lindsay

Ronald A. Lindsay is president and chief executive officer of the Center for Inquiry, a national, nonprofit organization devoted to the promotion of science and humanist values. He is also the author of Future Bioethics: Overcoming Taboos, Myths, and Dogmas.

The ability to use human embryos for medical research is an important public health issue, one that is continually denounced by religious zealots who claim that the embryo is entitled to the same rights as an adult human being. Such a claim is illogical and unscientific because an embryo is a mere grouping of cells and does not have an inherent capability of becoming a human being. Religious dogma aside, morally sound reasoning maintains that an embryo is not a human being, and embryonic stem cell research must be allowed to continue.

Just when you thought it was safe ... embryos are back in the news. A federal district court judge has issued an injunction [on August 23, 2010] blocking federal funding for research on embryonic stem cells [the injunction was temporarily lifted on September 28, 2010]. The judge ruled that federal funding would violate a 1996 law (the so-called Dickey Amendment) which prohibits funding of research that results in the destruction of embryos or subjects embryos to a risk of injury.

Ronald Lindsay, "Adult Reasoning About Embryos," The Center for Inquiry, centerfor inquiry.net, August 27, 2010. Reproduced by permission of Center for Inquiry.

I'm not going to analyze the judge's ruling in this case, other than to note that I believe it stands a good chance of being overturned because the judge did not give proper deference to the government agency (in this instance, the National Institutes of Health) responsible for interpreting and implementing the relevant law.

I'm more concerned with the beliefs of those who continue to oppose embryonic stem cell research. Those opposed to such research typically argue that the embryo is entitled to the same rights as an adult human being, which is why it should not be harmed in any way. They claim the embryo has the potential to develop into an adult human. Some even argue that the embryo has the inherent capacity to develop into an adult and will do so only if we leave it alone.

We do not and should not grant moral rights to mere groupings of cells.

Defining What an Embryo Actually Is

This is just religious dogma dressed up in pseudo-scientific garb. There are so many flaws in this reasoning that it is difficult to know where to begin, but here are some examples:

The early embryo is not an individual. Until about 14 days after conception, the embryo can divide into two or more parts. Under the right conditions, each of those parts can develop into a separate fetus. This is the phenomenon known as "twinning." Twinning shows that adult human beings are not identical with a previously existing zygote or embryo. If that were true, then each pair of twins would be identical with the same embryo. This is a logically incoherent position. If A and B are separate individuals, they cannot both be identical with a previously existent entity, C.

As the early embryo is not an individual, it cannot be the moral equivalent of an adult human. To claim that someone is harmed, there must be "someone" there. We do not and should not grant moral rights to mere groupings of cells.

The potential of the embryo does not make it a human person. Those who rely on the potential of the embryo to support their claim that it is morally equivalent to an adult human conveniently ignore the important role that extrinsic conditions play in embryonic and fetal development. An embryo in a petri dish is going nowhere. An embryo needs nutrients provided by the mother through the placenta in order to develop into a fetus and beyond. These nutrients regulate the epigenetic state of the embryo. The embryo does not have the inherent capability of expressing its potential on its own.

Additionally relevant to this discussion is the fact that embryos used in research are spare embryos from in vitro fertilization (IVF) procedures. In other words, they are embryos that are destined for the trash can, unless they are used in research. Therefore, they have no prospect of developing into a fetus. Their potential is no more than a theoretical construct.

The claim that the embryo is the moral equivalent of a human person is implicitly rejected by everyone. One important fact about embryonic development that is often overlooked is that between two-thirds and four-fifths of all embryos that are generated through standard sexual reproduction are spontaneously aborted. If embryos have the same status as human persons, this is a horrible tragedy and public health crisis that requires immediate and sustained attention. Not only should we abandon stem cell research, but we should reallocate the vast majority of our research dollars from projects such as cancer research into programs to help prevent this staggering loss of human life. Interestingly, none of the opponents of embryonic stem cell research have called for research programs that might increase the odds of embryo survival. Their failure to address this issue is puzzling if the embryo deserves the same moral respect as human persons.

Similarly, IVF, at least as currently practiced, would appear to be morally objectionable regardless of whether some embryos produced by this procedure are used in research. Those who utilize IVF intentionally create many embryos that they know will be discarded eventually. How can we accept a process that consigns entities that supposedly have the status of human persons to the rubbish bin?

The moral views of opponents are incoherent.

Separating Science from Religion

Finally, it is worth noting that the focus of the controversy over stem cell research is whether it should be federally funded, not whether it should be banned entirely (although there are some who have called for a ban). That we are even debating the wisdom of federal funding demonstrates that most of us—including the opponents of funding embryonic stem cell research—do not consider the embryo to have the same status as a human person. We do not debate the pros and cons of federal funding of research that would destroy adult humans.

Consideration of these implications of the position that embryos are entitled to the same rights as human persons demonstrates that this position cannot be reconciled with widely accepted views—including the views of opponents of funding embryonic stem cell research. Of course, this does not "prove" that this position is morally unsound. It merely establishes that the moral views of opponents are incoherent.

At the end of the day, we know what is at work here. Those holding the embryo sacred are implicitly making use of religiously inspired ensoulment doctrines; that is, a soul is what makes us special and a soul enters the zygote at the moment of conception. Unfortunately, in the 21st century we still find ourselves in thrall to religious dogma on an important public health issue.

We can only hope that some day humanity will grow up, leave its religious infancy behind, and reason as adults about moral issues.

5

Stem Cell Research Should Be Federally Funded

Michael Rugnetta and Michael Peroski

Michael Rugnetta is a research assistant with the Progressive Bioethics Initiative at the Center for American Progress, a public policy research and advocacy organization headquartered in Washington, D.C. Michael Peroski is a former intern with the Progressive Bioethics Initiative at the Center for American Progress and biochemistry student at Allegheny College in Pennsylvania.

If US scientists are to create vital new therapeutic medicine, they must be able to study human embryonic stem cells. Embryonic stem cells are considered "master cells" because of their capability to transform into any cell in the body, and are also considered the "gold standard" against which all other stem cells—including adult stem cells—must be compared. In order for America to remain a global scientific leader and keep up in the biomedical field, embryonic stem cell research must be federally funded and legislated in such a way that future administrations cannot obstruct the research. Additionally, the government should create oversight guidelines to ensure embryonic stem cell research operates under cautious and ethical standards.

It is time for the United States to stake its claim as the world leader in regenerative medicine, which promises to become a vital component of the cutting edge of life sciences research

Michael Rugnetta and Michael Peroski, "A Life Sciences Crucible: Stem Cell Research and Innovation Done Responsibly and Ethically," pp. 2–5, Center for American Progress, January 2009. This material was created by the Center for American Progress (www.americanprogress.org). Reproduced by permission.

and innovation in the 21st century. To ensure research in this newly emerging field of life sciences is conducted responsibly and ethically, the federal government must reform its stem cell research policy in order to fund embryonic stem cell research that is robust and comprehensive as well as cautious and principled.

The Potential of Regenerative Medicine

Regenerative medicine is a new therapeutic approach that works by cultivating a small sample of a patient's own cells, reprogramming them, and using them to heal the patient without the risk of rejection or severe side effects that usually result from introducing foreign therapeutic materials. The potential therapies range from transforming the pancreatic cells of diabetics so they can produce insulin to reconnecting the nerves in severed spinal cords. Indeed, there have already been some modest clinical applications where heart muscles and cartilage have been repaired with stem cells derived from bone marrow.

But that is just the tip of the iceberg. The greatest potential for regenerative medicine lies in scientists' ability to tap into the process of cell differentiation and development. This can only be achieved by tracing the development of human cells from the very beginning. To do so, scientists need to conduct research on embryonic stem cells so that they can discover how these all-purpose cells can change into any one of the more than 200 different cell types in the human body.

Moreover, by studying the development of embryonic stem cells scientists will be able to discover how the human genome goes about manifesting itself and creating unique individual persons. These efforts will provide us with unprecedented insights into human development, how it can go wrong, and how it can be fixed.

Opponents of embryonic stem cell research argue that there have been many scientific advances made using stem cells that do not come from embryos, such as bone marrow-derived stem cells, which are a type of adult stem cell. Opponents also point to so-called induced pluripotent stem cells, which are created when adult cells—say, skin cells—are reprogrammed to become all-purpose "pluripotent" cells. These arguments are valid, but only up to a point. The reason: embryonic stem cells are both the original "master cells" capable of turning into any cell in the body as well as the "gold standard" against which all other stem cells must be compared.

The Magnitude of Embryonic Stem Cells

Scientists determine whether other types of stem cells hold the promise of delivering the kinds of regenerative medicine envisioned by life scientists by analyzing the surfaces of these alternative cells to see whether they have the same proteins and therefore the same capabilities as embryonic stem cells. Evidence suggests that these stem cell-specific proteins activate certain chemical pathways in the stem cells, which in turn allow them to maintain their pluripotency. Regardless of what type of stem cells prove to be the most useful, this process of embryonic stem cell comparison must be carried out for each therapeutic application, whether for Alzheimer's disease, Parkinson's disease, spinal cord injuries, or any of the other myriad conditions for which stem cell therapy might be possible.

The bottom line is that embryonic stem cell research is good science.

Just as important: embryonic stem cells must be studied so that scientists can learn more about developmental biology. It is a longstanding research paradigm to study failures of development by determining when, where, and how genes malfunction. The ultimate goal is to develop a guidebook that will tell us exactly how each gene or combination of genes contributes to the development of a unique individual. This will greatly enhance our understanding of basic genetics and could allow scientists to develop drugs that can prevent the diseases from developing in the first place.

Additionally, embryonic stem cells can aid in the refinement of these new drugs since the cells can be differentiated into specific cell types upon which scientists can quickly test whether a drug has a desired effect. This will make the drug development process and then the clinical trial process much safer and more efficient.

The bottom line is that embryonic stem cell research is good science. It is necessary science, and it needs to be part of America's federally funded biomedical research enterprise if America is to retain its status as a global scientific leader. That's why embryonic stem cell research must be conducted responsibly and ethically, and why the incoming [Barack] Obama administration must outline new federal research and funding oversight guidelines for embryonic stem cell research that are cautious and principled.

The Inclusion of Ethical Guidelines

The first step toward renewing U.S. life sciences leadership must be taken by the executive branch. President Barack Obama has the option of either issuing an executive order or issuing a presidential memorandum to govern stem cell research. Either way, the primary objective of the executive document must be to lift the existing temporal restriction on the federal funding of embryonic stem cell research.

Currently, federal funding is only available for research on the 21 lines of embryonic stem cells that were derived before August 9, 2001. Once this arbitrary limit is lifted, the National Institutes of Health will be able to issue grants to scientists who wish to research embryonic stem cells in accordance with guidelines for ethically derived cells, including:

- The stem cells must come from embryos that were originally created at *in vitro* fertilization [IVF] clinics for the purpose of fertility treatment but are now stored at these IVF clinics because more were created than required to fulfill the patient's clinical need.

- Proper written informed consent is obtained from the donors.

- As part of the informed consent process, the embryo donors along with the physician determine that the embryos will never be implanted in a womb and would otherwise be destroyed.

- There are no financial inducements and the donors understand the purpose of the research is not to eventually confer therapeutic benefits upon the donors.

Embryonic stem cell research requirements along these lines should also be codified in legislation by the incoming 111th Congress and become law so that future presidents cannot obstruct this research.

In addition, it is current policy that no embryonic stem cells will be derived using federal funds. Federal funds will only pay for research on stem cells that have already been derived with private funds.

To enforce these ethical guidelines and to ensure that all stem cell research (embryonic or otherwise) is conducted cautiously and responsibly so as not to threaten the safety or autonomy of research subjects or the donors of research materials, the following administrative oversight requirements should be included either in the president's document or in legislation that should be passed in the first session of the 111th Congress:

- The National Institutes of Health [NIH] should require that all research be conducted under the review of a stem cell research oversight committee that adheres to

6

Stem Cell Research Should Be Privately Funded

Sigrid Fry-Revere and Molly Elgin

Sigrid Fry-Revere is the founder and president of the Center for Ethical Solutions, a nonprofit public policy organization dedicated to the principles of free enterprise and limited government. Prior to starting the Center, Fry-Revere was the director of bioethics studies at the Cato Institute. Molly Elgin assisted Fry-Revere in research for an article on legal trends in bioethics, published in the Journal of Clinical Ethics *in 2007.*

Research using human embryonic stem cells has shown great promise in developing cures for chronic and degenerative diseases, such as cancer and Parkinson's disease. Stem cell research projects, however, are also inherently speculative and ethically controversial, and taxpayers—especially averse taxpayers— should not be forced to pay for them. Much of the success from embryonic research has resulted from private funding; for example, in vitro *fertilization research was developed without any government funding. Furthermore, political regulations and moral disputes hinder the expeditious advancement of stem cell research. The sensible resolution is for stem cell research to be privately funded.*

The United States Congress and more than 28 state legislatures have considered spending billions of taxpayer dollars on stem cell research over the next few years. The National In-

Sigrid Fry-Revere and Molly Elgin, "Public Stem Cell Research Funding: Boon or Boondoggle?" pp. 3–5; 14–18, Competitive Enterprise Institute, CEI.org, September 2008. Reproduced by permission of Competitive Enterprise Institute.

stitutes of Health (NIH) has already committed billions. Though debates rage over the ethics of the work, a more fundamental question is being ignored: Is stem cell research a sensible expenditure of taxpayer dollars? This is not a question of whether the research should be conducted, but whether *public* funding for it is justified.

Because stem cell research is inherently speculative and politically controversial, the public would be best served if governments left it to the private sector. Politicians who promise cures in the near future for cancer and Parkinson's disease, lower future health care costs, and a booming biotechnology economy are being disingenuous. Each stem cell project is highly speculative, and it is not the place of government to gamble with taxpayers' money.

Furthermore, there is little risk that stem cell research will go unfunded—biotech companies, philanthropic organizations, and individuals have already invested billions of dollars in such research, and they show no sign of stopping. More importantly, the politicized nature of public debates over stem cell research threaten to spill over into and disrupt the research itself. The prospect of public funding so angers some Americans that it has spurred movements to restrict *private* stem cell research efforts. Under such circumstances, government funding for stem cell research is more hindrance than help to the advancement of science.

The Political Controversy

In November 2007, New Jersey voters rejected an initiative to borrow $450 million to fund state-run stem cell research. Defeat should not have come as a surprise. New Jersey voters had the advantage of seeing how little California's 2004 stem cell funding initiative has accomplished at an extremely high cost. New Jerseyites have also seen the flourishing of private stem cell research efforts in their own backyard, evidence that such research need not depend on government funding. Moreover, it simply makes no sense for a state with the highest per-capita public debt in the nation to borrow still more money to spend on stem cell research.

Yet some New Jersey legislators remain eager to increase taxes and spending to finance stem cell research—and they are not alone. By the end of 2008, the National Institutes of Health will have spent over $2.5 billion on stem cell research in just five years. Nine states, including California, New York, and Connecticut, have committed to combined spending of over $4.1 billion over the next 10 years. Government funding advocates consistently downplay the significant financial risks involved in the research and the inefficiency of public programs in managing its progress. They also seem to ignore the fact that private companies are doing just fine conducting stem cell research without government help or interference.

New Jersey voters were wise to learn from California's mistakes, and residents of others states would be wise to follow suit. Most of the problems that arose in California are endemic to government-run efforts in general, such as wasted time and money and political squabbling over the fair distribution of funds. This is not to suggest that private initiatives cannot be wasteful, inefficient, or unsuccessful—many biotechnology firms fail because they are high-risk ventures. But in the private sector individuals make their investments voluntarily. If people find that they have been lured into investing their money under false pretenses, they have legal remedies available to address such injustices, including opportunities for reparations. There are no such remedies for mistakes made at the ballot box. Whether or not stem cell research proves a worthy investment on the whole, citizens of other states would be wise to follow New Jersey's example and reject any proposal for government funding of stem cell research.

Stem Cells and What They Can Do

To understand this issue, it is worth learning a little about the underlying science. Most cells perform only one function, and they can only produce other cells of the same type, which, like the original cells, will eventually mature and die. For example, newly divided muscle cells become mature muscle cells, and they can only produce new muscle cells. However, unlike most cells, stem cells can generate different types of cells and regenerate continuously. When a stem cell divides, one daughter cell becomes a specialized cell, such as a muscle or blood cell, while the other daughter cell remains a stem cell, which then can produce the same or another kind of cell, again leaving a daughter cell behind to continue the stem line. Thus, stem cells can give rise to both specialized and unspecialized cells.

Different types of stem cells differ in the variety of cells they can produce. Adult stem cells are already being tested for the treatment of heart disease, rheumatoid arthritis, Parkinson's disease, type one diabetes, advanced kidney cancer, and spinal injury. Cord blood stem cell transplants are used in therapies for leukemias and lymphomas. And, in at least one experiment in mice, the onset of a form of Tay-Sachs disease was delayed by injecting the mice with stem cells taken from human embryonic stem cells. Embryonic stem cells are clearly the most versatile of stem cells, though research remains in a very early stage. Indeed, scientists have not yet been consistently able to control the growth of embryonic stem cells; their interactions with other cells often cause unpredictable growth patterns, including tumors, and tissue rejection responses. Efforts to reprogram adult cells to act more like embryonic stem cells give hope to those who oppose the use of human embryos in research, but the reprogramming of adult stem cells has implementation problems of its own.

Scientists have worked with stem cells since the 1960s, but, in 1998, University of Wisconsin biophysics professor James Thomson discovered human embryonic stem cells and their unspecialized, self-renewing nature. In December 1999, the journal *Science* declared human embryonic stem cell research "the breakthrough of the year." The potential applications of Thomson's discovery stirred not only the imagination of the scientific community, but also that of millions of people who hoped embryonic stem cell therapies could help them or their loved ones overcome dreaded diseases.

Embryonic stem cell research holds extraordinary promise, but its potential therapeutic applications are still speculative. Until scientists can control the growth of stem cells and make them interact with other cells without causing tumors or rejection responses in patients, there is very little therapeutic use for embryonic stem cells. As the public liaison of the National Institute of Neurological Disorders and Stroke put it, "[embryonic stem cell] research is in its infancy. There are many technical and scientific hurdles to overcome, and it will probably be years before the results of any such studies in humans that may be developed are known. Currently, the usefulness of embryonic stem cells to treat disease, even in animal models, is still far from clear." . . .

Historical Example of Private Funding Success

Given the risks and questionable benefits, why are state governments rushing to fund stem cell research? Some argue that, precisely because of the risky nature of the work, private companies will either not pursue it or will only focus on the more immediately profitable aspects. These claims are false. The riskiness of cutting-edge research methods and technologies is standard in the biotechnology industry and is therefore unlikely to intimidate investors whose financing of the biotech industry totaled over $20 billion in 2005. The more pressing risks hindering greater private investment are political controversy and the threat of stifling regulation.

Private funding continues to be vital to stem cell research. In fact, the most important breakthrough in the field, James

Thomson's discovery of the nature of human embryonic stem cells, was the result of privately funded research. And Thomson's discovery utilized embryos derived from *in vitro* fertilization (IVF) clinics, another private funding success story.

To understand the possibilities of private research funding, an actual historical success story provides a good illustration. In the 1970s and 1980s, scientists lobbied the federal government to support research on new reproductive technologies, but ethical concerns regarding experimentation on human embryos stymied their efforts. Research advocates spent millions of dollars trying to convince the President, Congress, and the National Institutes of Health that funding research involving *in vitro* fertilization techniques was crucial for the United States to maintain its position as a leader in reproductive medicine. Advocates of public funding for IVF argued that a "brain drain" would ensue, and that infertile Americans would have to go abroad for the reproductive health care they should be receiving at home.

Eventually, public research funding advocates lost that debate. No human IVF research was ever federally funded, and there is no evidence it has been funded by any U.S. state. But, as the divisive debate over experimenting on human embryos and the ethical merits of "test-tube babies" raged in the headlines, a number of researchers quietly continued their work with private funds. Far from suffering a brain drain, within a short time, the United States overtook the United Kingdom, its leading competitor in IVF research. Today in the United States, IVF for humans is estimated as a $3 billion a year industry—all of it developed without any government funding. . . .

More Is Not Necessarily Better

Some proponents of government funding of stem cell research argue that more is better, and that there is no reason not to pursue both federal and private funding simultaneously. However, there is evidence that government spending "crowds out" private contributors. The Congressional Budget Office (CBO) made exactly this point in a report on research and development in the pharmaceutical industry. "Even as it produces substantial social benefits," the CBO observed, government spending "on basic research and development can also discourage private investment." Government can discourage private investment directly, "as when the government sponsors research that the private sector would otherwise have conducted," or indirectly, as when "the government competes for trained scientists and other scarce resources and bids up their prices." The results are reduced private investment and lower long-term growth.

Compared to the troubles facing public funding, privately funded stem cell research has an impressive record of proven successes.

In fact, public funding can actually have a negative influence, if the political repercussions lead to increased and confusing regulation and limitations. For example, a bill in Nebraska banning cloning for reproductive purposes has been amended to include bans on cloning for research purposes, which would essentially outlaw human embryonic stem cell research regardless of how it is funded. Nebraska Right to Life Executive Director Julie Schmit-Albin expressed concern that the original bill "could have emboldened private sector cloning labs to come into Nebraska and we are thankful it was removed." In Missouri, the Stowers Institute for Medical Research feared the imposition of restrictions enough to put on hold its planned expansion in Kansas City and invest in other states instead. Reliance on private funding alone would tend to de-politicize the process.

Compared to the troubles facing public funding, privately funded stem cell research has an impressive record of proven successes and breakthroughs. Before Thomson's discovery, human embryo research relied exclusively on private funding because no public funding was available. Yet, Thomson was not the only one doing research on human embryonic stem cells in the 1990s, and many more entered the field after he published his findings in 1998. For example, in 2001, Harvard University, the Howard Hughes Medical Institute, the Juvenile Diabetes Research Foundation, and Boston IVF began a collaborative human embryonic stem cell research project, and by early 2004 they had developed 17 new human embryonic stem cell lines without any government assistance. They began their research months before President [George W.] Bush allowed very limited funding for research on existing stem cell lines, four years before California's stem cell funding initiative was even on the ballot, and almost seven years before California issued the first bonds authorized by Proposition 71.

Quicker and More Effective Results

While the California Institute for Regenerative Medicine deals with disputes over the disbursement of funds, private contributions by investors and philanthropists continue to advance stem cell research. The adult stem cell product market—which experienced an increase of over 100 percent from 2006 to 2007—is testament to the quicker and more effective results produced by private industry. Today, the most politically controversial form of stem cell research, embryonic stem cell research, is still almost exclusively supported by private funds. But substantial amounts of private funding are also available for adult stem cell and cord blood stem cell research. . . .

Were stem cell research to be conducted exclusively in the private sector, those who see its funding as important could donate their own money and urge others do the same. At the same time, those who discount the urgency, see such research as a waste of resources, or consider it immoral, can try to convince others not to support it. Best of all, such debates can take place without getting bogged down in political struggles over whether or not it is appropriate for government to provide financial support for the research. A free market of ideas, with a plurality of private funding sources, in the long run will result in less waste and more funds being directed to those most vested in solving shared research concerns.

7

Federal Funds Would Be Better Spent on Adult Stem Cell Research

Michael Fumento

Michael Fumento is an attorney, investigative reporter, and public speaker who specializes in science and health issues. He is the author of several books, including BioEvolution: How Biotechnology Is Changing Our World *and* Science Under Siege.

Since 1998, human embryonic stem cell researchers and lobbyists have claimed to be on the verge of developing cures and treatments for many debilitating diseases, yet no treatments or cures have come forth. Adult stem cells, on the other hand, currently treat over seventy diseases and have the potential to cure even more. Additionally, embryonic stem cells are much more difficult to work with in laboratories than adult stem cells, and have a tendency to form into tumors. It seems obvious that the federal funding that has been—and is being—squandered on embryonic stem cell research would be more beneficially spent on research using adult stem cells.

If you or a loved one is currently ill or planning to be so anytime in the near future, don't bother looking to embryonic stem cell (ESC) research to help. Instead, you need to consult the adult stem cell (ASC) literature whereupon you'll find these little guys currently treat or cure over 70 diseases and conditions even as they're involved in almost 1,300 human clinical trials.

Michael Fumento, "Adult Approaches: Will Embryonic Stem Cell Promise Ever Pay Off?" *The American Spectator*, Vol. 40, Issue 4, May 2007, pp. 52–55. Reproduced by permission of *The American Spectator*.

Embryonic Stem Cell Conjecture

At this point, all that ESCs hold is promise. They are used in no treatments, cures, or human clinical trials. They *are* used in raising false hopes and hence money. The University of California, Irvine's Hans Keirstead, who claims to have used ESCs to cure paralyzed rats, said last year [2006] he would start human clinical trials this year. Problem is, he's been saying "next year" since 2002. Check your calendar. Moreover—and this is typical of ESC researcher grandstanding—his rats weren't even paralyzed. Rather, as opposed to what he tells reporters, including the late Ed Bradley on [the television news program] *60 Minutes*, the injuries were "moderate in severity [and] sparing some hind limb motor function," as he reported in a medical journal.

ESC lobbyists sniff that ASC research got a big head start. "Researchers began using adult stem cells from bone marrow back in 1960," claims Religioustolerance.org on its website. (Note that the very name furthers the ESC lobby's goal of portraying all their opponents as religious fanatics.) "It was only in 1998 that other researchers were able to isolate and cultivate embryo stem cells. Adult stem cell research thus has an almost four decade head start compared to embryo-derived stem cells."

While ASCs were originally identified in marrow, now they've been found throughout the body.

In fact, ASCs and ESCs were both discovered in rodents in the 1950s. But the ASCs—from marrow—were readily adaptable for treating leukemia and other human blood disorders. ESCs, conversely, precisely because of their much-touted flexibility, were so hard to work with that it wasn't until 1998, in the lab of the University of Wisconsin's James Thomson, that the first human line of ESCs was created. They remain a real bear to work with, which is why their domain remains primarily the Petri dish.

But what is the ESC promise and when will these cells and scientists deliver?

New Developments from Adult Stem Cells

Since they are mere days old, ESCs are so malleable as to lend themselves to becoming mature cells from all three germ layers of the human body—about 220 types of cells total. ASCs, because they are more developed, were long thought to be considerably less flexible. That is, you could get marrow from marrow stem cells along with blood, muscle, and an amazing array of other types of mature cells. But you couldn't get neurons or pancreatic cells because those are in different germ layers.

But two developments have eaten away at this apparent ESC advantage.

The first is that while ASCs were originally identified in marrow, now they've been found throughout the body including skin, brains, spinal cords, dental pulp, muscles, blood vessels, corneas, retinas, livers, hair follicles, and umbilical cords. Fat, America's most inexhaustible resource, contains stem cells that have been converted into more fat (for cosmetic purposes), bone, cartilage, and nerve cells. Importantly, nerve cells are in a different germ layer from fat.

With numerous types of stem cells in all three germ layers, it's possible we could constitute all 220 cell types (assuming you even *need* all 220 cell types) without a one-size-fits all ES cell.

The second development is that since 2002 researchers have been discovering ASCs that apparently can be converted to mature cells in all three germ layers, beginning with the University of Minnesota Stem Cell Institute Catherine Verfaillie's finding, announced in *Nature* magazine. Others have since used different types of cells than she did, but to the same effect.

The most exciting news in this area lately has been the revelation, announced in January, of Anthony Atala. Atala, a physician and director of the Institute for Regenerative Medicine at Wake Forest University School of Medicine, found that stem cells in the amniotic fluid that fill the sac surrounding the fetus appear to be just as versatile as ESCs. As he told [television network] PBS's *Online NewsHour*, "We have been able to drive the cell to what we call all three germ layers, which basically means all three major classes of tissues available in the body, from which all cells come from."

One advantage of ESCs has been that most types of adult stem cells cannot be multiplied outside of the body for very long; embryonic ones may replicate in the lab indefinitely. But Atala's amniotic stem cells grow as fast outside the body as ESCs (doubling every 36 hours), and he's now been growing the same cell line for two years with no indication of slowing.

Downplaying Adult Stem Cell Successes

ESC researchers have desperately tried to downplay these findings, to the extent that *The New York Times*, which told readers three years ago [2004] that there were *no* cures or treatments involving ASCs, refused to even mention Atala's work. *Newsweek International* did make note of it but claimed, "Many scientists are quick to emphasize that comprehensive human trials are still many years away."

The ASC advantage in therapies grows by the month.

The magazine is correct only if "years away" means "years ago." As Atala himself has noted, amniotic stem cells are identical to placental stem cells. The *New England Journal of Medicine* carried one paper on a placenta stem cell trial back in 1996 and another paper two years later. There's been an ongoing clinical trial since 2001 to treat sickle cell anemia.

Backers of more funding for ESC research are also quick to point out that Atala himself, after his article was published, wrote in a letter: "It is essential that National Institute[s] of Health [NIH]-funded researchers are able to fully pursue embryonic stem cell research." But as I observed two years ago, ASC researchers almost always say something like that after making a breakthrough. NIH is the hand that feeds them and NIH likes handing checks to ESC researchers. There's also nothing to be gained by angering colleagues whose livelihoods are based on tinkering with ESCs, if not actually accomplishing anything.

ESCs certainly had a head start in the race to develop all types of cells from a single one. But that gap has either been rapidly narrowed or even erased. Meanwhile the ASC advantage in therapies grows by the month.

Which leaves us with a final but very important question. When will the ESC promise pay off? When can we expect something more from them than arcane articles in medical journals (though repeatedly portrayed as miracle breakthroughs in *The New York Times*)? You know, like, well, actually making sick people better?

The standard answer is in about a decade, which must be true because it's been "in about a decade" for years now. Yes widen, lengthen and deepen that federal trough enough and toss in lots of state funding from places like California (3 billion bucks over ten years) and we just might be able to do with an ESC in 2017 what we can with an ASC today. But one leading ESC scientist says even that may be far too optimistic. That scientist is none other than the University of Wisconsin's James Thomson himself.

Obstacles to Embryonic Stem Cell Research

In addressing a convention in February, Thomson pointed out that obstacles to therapeutic ESC research are daunting. Among them is that ES cells require the recipient to permanently use dangerous immunosuppressive drugs and that they have a nasty tendency to form into teratomas—which means "monster tumor." Said Thomson, "I don't want to sound too pessimistic because this is all doable, but it's going to be very hard." Further, "It's likely to take a long time." How long? The *Associated Press* writer characterized it as "likely decades away." That's a minimum of 20 years, with no maximum.

As to what we can expect from those therapies, as the *AP* writer quoting Thomson put it: "One day, some believe the [embryonic stem] cells will become sources of brain tissue, muscle and bone marrow to replace diseased or injured body parts." In other words, they'll be able to do what ASCs do right now. Muscle? In the last few years, doctors have used ASCs to rebuild hearts and livers not in Petri dishes but in live humans. Marrow? As noted, marrow stem cells have been curing people for half a century.

Finally, neuronal stem cells have treated brain diseases like Parkinsonism in animal models and assuredly will soon enter human testing. Not soon enough, to be sure, but certainly a lot earlier than "decades." Autopsies on bone marrow recipients have found that some of the cells made their way to the brain and became nerve cells. Whether this was actually therapeutic remains unknown. So let's just give the ESC researchers all the money they want for their decades-away promise, mindful that those funds could have gone to ASC research projects treating and curing humans today. Then perhaps they'll announce that, given enough money and perhaps decades, they'll also build a computer with the processing power of a dime-store calculator.

8

Human Embryo Cloning Should Be Banned

William L. Saunders

William L. Saunders is senior vice president of legal affairs at Americans United for Life (AUL) and served as senior fellow and director of the Family Research Council's Center for Human Life and Bioethics. He has written extensively on bioethics and human dignity, including "The Human Embryo in Debate," a chapter in the book Human Dignity in the Biotech Century.

History has shown that experimentation using human subjects—even if touted as being in the interests of "the greater good"—can be brutal, dehumanizing, and ultimately immoral. During World II, for example, the Nazis performed scientific experiments on Jews, Poles, and gypsies because they considered these people to be inferior and unworthy of human dignity. After the war, the Nuremberg Code was created to establish ethical guidelines for the civilized world so that such atrocities against human beings would not happen again. The Nuremberg Code remains relevant today with regard to the subject of human embryo cloning. Therapeutic cloning creates an embryo only to destroy it and harvest its stem cells. Because the human embryo is a living human being, such experimentation destroys innocent human life and violates the ethical standards set forth in the Nuremberg Code.

William L. Saunders, "Human Cloning and the Abuse of Science," Family Research Council, 2007, pp. 10–17. Reproduced by permission of Family Research Council.

Cloning indisputably destroys innocent human life. This basic truth should lead the world to reject human cloning. However, in an effort to extricate human cloning from this ethical vise grip, its supporters attempt to draw a distinction between human life, which begins at conception, and human "personhood," which begins only at their say-so.

The Nuremberg Code

Unfortunately, the arbitrary denial of "personhood" to human beings has a long and cruel history. The Nuremberg Code, formulated in the years after World War II, is particularly instructive with regard to the current debate on human cloning. For instance, when the principal author of the report on human cloning issued by the National Academy of Sciences testified before the President's Council on Bioethics, he stated that "reproductive cloning" would violate the Nuremberg Code: "The Nuremberg Code, with which I am in full agreement, outlines those kinds of things you would not simply [do] for the sake of knowledge that involve human subjects."

The Nuremberg Code is a body of ethical norms enunciated by the Nuremberg Tribunal, which, after World War II, had the responsibility of judging the actions of the Nazis and their allies. The point of the code was to restate and apply the established ethical norms of the civilized world.

Nazi laws had defined Jews and other "undesirables" as non-persons. Eventually, between six and nine million of these "undesirables" were sent to extermination camps and killed. However, before the killing in the camps began, the Nazis had engaged in an extensive campaign of euthanasia against the mentally and physically handicapped, which not only foreshadowed but also prepared the way for the extermination camps. In his book *The Nazi Doctors*, Robert Jay Lifton draws our attention to a book titled *The Permission to Destroy Life Unworthy of Life*, written during the campaign. Lifton writes:

[It was] published in 1920 and written jointly by two ... German professors: the jurist Karl Binding ... and Alfred Hoche, professor of psychiatry at the University of Freiburg. Carefully argued in the numbered-paragraph form of the traditional philosophical treatise, the book included as "unworthy life" not only the incurably ill but large segments of the mentally ill, the feebleminded, and retarded and deformed children. . . . [T]he authors professionalized and medicalized the entire concept; destroying life unworthy of life was "purely a healing treatment" and a "healing" work.

There is to be no experimentation on a human subject when it is known that death or disabling injury will result.

The Nazis were determined to "cleanse" the genetic pool to produce "better" Aryans. Nazi officials announced that "under the direction of specialists ... all therapeutic possibilities will be administered according to the latest scientific knowledge." The result of this therapeutic treatment of "inferior" lives was that "eventually a network of some thirty killing areas within existing institutions was set up throughout Germany and in Austria and Poland." In their book, *The Nazi Doctors and The Nuremberg Code*, George Annas and Michael Grodin reveal that:

At the same time that forced sterilization and abortion were instituted for individuals of "inferior" genetic stock, sterilization and abortion for healthy German women were declared illegal and punishable (in some cases by death) as a "crime against the German body." As one might imagine, Jews and others deemed racially suspect were exempted from these restrictions. On November 10, 1938, a Luneberg court legalized abortion for Jews. A decree of June 23, 1943, allowed for abortions for Polish workers, but only if they were not judged "racially valuable."

cause each of us to think deeply about whether there is any essential difference between the reality of those Nazi experiments and "therapeutic cloning." As we have shown, each case involves a living human being, and that human being is killed in the aim of a perceived "higher" good.

Cloning proponents try to distinguish between the two cases by saying that the cloned human being has no "potential." But in each case, it is the actions of other human beings that rob the first of "potential" (in the first case, the actions of Nazi executioners; in the second, the laboratory technicians). In either case, the human subject is full of potential simply by being a living human being. Of course, almost miraculously, many of the inmates of the camps did survive when the allies rescued them. Equally miraculously, frozen embryos have been implanted in a woman's womb and brought to live (and healthy) birth.

As we have shown, every embryo is not merely "potentially" a life, but actual life, a human being from the first moment of existence. Furthermore, any living human embryo has the inherent "potential" to develop into a healthy baby. It is disingenuous for supporters of cloning to claim the cloned human embryo is only "potential life" because they plan to mandate by law that it be destroyed before it can come to birth. Regardless of its location, the human embryo, by its nature, is full of potential, unless the actions of adult human beings deprive it of the opportunity to realize that potential.

Alexander Solzhenitsyn [Russian historian and novelist sentenced to a labor camp for writing anti-Soviet propaganda], a man who chronicled and suffered under another ideology that denied the dignity of each and every human being, observed, "Gradually it was disclosed to me that the line separating good and evil passes not through states, nor between classes, nor between political parties either, but right though every human heart, and through all human hearts. This line shifts. Inside us, it oscillates."

Solzhenitsyn did not regard the perpetrators of brutal crimes in his own country as inhuman monsters. Rather, he saw the essential truth—they were human beings, engaged in immoral acts. They engaged in those acts by dehumanizing the persons on whom their brutality was inflicted, and they did so in the name of (perhaps in the passionate belief in) a greater good. But Solzhenitsyn reminds us that, unless we are willing to admit that, for the best as well as for the worst of motives, we are also capable of inhuman acts, we will have no guard against committing them. No one is safe from brutality so long as we think that it is only inhuman others who are capable of inhuman acts. Rather, we will be secure when we are willing to look honestly at the objective reality of our acts, while realizing that we, too, are capable of acts that violate the inherent dignity of another, and refuse to engage in such acts despite the good we believe would result from those acts. In the debate over the cloning and destruction of embryonic human beings, this essential truth must be our guide.

9

Therapeutic Cloning of Human Embryos Should Be Allowed

Michael J. Sandel

Michael J. Sandel is an American political philosopher and a professor at Harvard University. He also teaches the seminar "Ethics and Biotechnology," which considers the ethical implications of several biotechnological procedures and possibilities.

The main objection to embryonic stem cell research revolves around the moral belief that destroying a human embryo is in actuality destroying a human being. A question then arises regarding whether it is morally permissible to use excess embryos left over from fertility treatments, as opposed to using cloned embryos created specifically for research. Surely, creating embryos for the treatment and cure of debilitating diseases is just as morally acceptable as creating embryos for treating infertility. The ethical dilemma of using human embryos for research is understandable; however, creating clusters of cells to cure disease, all the while following strict ethical guidelines, shows a virtuous and reverent appreciation of life and should be allowed.

The debate over stem cell research poses three questions. First, should embryonic stem cell research be permitted? Second, should it be funded by the government? Third, should it matter, for either permissibility or funding, whether the

ported stem cell research on leftover embryos created for reproduction, but not on embryos created for research. The stem cell funding bill voted by Congress (and vetoed by President [George W.] Bush) in 2006 also made this distinction; it would have funded stem cell research only on embryos left over from fertility treatments.

Curing diseases such as Parkinson's and diabetes is at least as important as treating infertility.

Beyond its appeal as a political compromise, this distinction seems morally defensible as well. On closer examination, however, it does not hold up. The distinction fails because it begs the question of whether the "spare" embryos should be created in the first place. To see how this is so, imagine a fertility clinic that accepts egg and sperm donations for two purposes—reproduction and stem cell research. No cloning is involved. The clinic creates two groups of embryos, one from eggs and sperm donated for the purpose of IVF [in vitro fertilization], the other from eggs and sperm donated by people who want to advance the cause of stem cell research.

Which group of embryos may an ethical scientist use for stem cell research? Those who agree with Frist and Romney are left in a paradoxical position: They would permit the scientist to use spare embryos from the first group (since they were created for reproduction and will otherwise be discarded) but not from the second group (since they were deliberately created for research). In fact, Frist and Romney have both sought to ban the deliberate creation of embryos in IVF clinics for purposes of research.

Treating Disease Is Just as Worthy as Treating Infertility

The paradoxical scenario brings out the flaw in the compromise position: Those who oppose the creation of embryos for stem cell research but support research on IVF "spares" fail to address the morality of in vitro fertilization itself. If it is immoral to create and sacrifice embryos for the sake of curing or treating devastating diseases, why isn't it also objectionable to create and discard spare embryos in the course of treating infertility? Or, to look at the argument from the opposite end, if the creation and sacrifice of embryos in IVF is morally acceptable, why isn't the creation and sacrifice of embryos for stem cell research also acceptable? After all, both practices serve worthy ends, and curing diseases such as Parkinson's and diabetes is at least as important as treating infertility.

Those who see a moral difference between the sacrifice of embryos in IVF and the sacrifice of embryos in stem cell research might reply as follows: The fertility doctor who creates excess embryos does so to increase the odds of a successful pregnancy; he does not know which embryos will ultimately be discarded, and does not intend the death of any. But the scientist who deliberately creates an embryo for stem cell research knows the embryo will die, for to carry out the research it is necessary to destroy the embryo. Charles Krauthammer [American syndicated columnist], who favors stem cell research on IVF spares but not on embryos created for research, put the point sharply: "The bill that would legalize research cloning essentially sanctions . . . a most ghoulish enterprise: the creation of nascent human life for the sole purpose of its exploitation and destruction."

This reply is unpersuasive, for two reasons. First, the claim that creating embryos for stem cell research amounts to creating life *for the purpose of* exploiting or destroying it is misleading. The destruction of the embryo is, admittedly, a foreseeable consequence of the act, but the purpose is curing disease. Those who create embryos for research no more aim at destruction or exploitation than those who create embryos for fertility treatments aim at discarding spares.

Second, although fertility doctors and patients do not know in advance which of the embryos they create will wind up being discarded, the fact remains that IVF, as practiced in the United States, generates tens of thousands of excess embryos bound for destruction. (A recent study found that some 400,000 frozen embryos are languishing in American fertility clinics, with another 52,000 in the United Kingdom and 71,000 in Australia.) It is true that, once these doomed embryos exist, "nothing is lost" if they are used for research. But whether they should be created in the first place is as much a policy choice as whether to permit the creation of embryos for research. German federal law, for example, regulates fertility clinics and prohibits doctors from fertilizing more eggs than will be implanted at any one time. As a result, German IVF clinics do not generate excess embryos. The existence of large numbers of doomed embryos in the freezers of U.S. fertility clinics is not an unalterable fact of nature but the consequence of a policy that elected officials could change if they wanted to. So far, however, few of those who would ban the creation of embryos for research have called for a ban on the creation and destruction of excess embryos in fertility clinics.

If cloning for stem cell research violates the respect the embryo is due, then . . . so does any fertility treatment that creates and discards excess embryos.

Whoever is right about the moral status of the embryo, one thing is clear: Opponents of research cloning cannot have it both ways. They cannot endorse the creation and destruction of excess embryos in fertility clinics, or the use of such embryos in research, and at the same time complain that creating embryos for research and regenerative medicine is morally objectionable. If cloning for stem cell research violates the respect the embryo is due, then so does stem cell research on IVF spares, and so does any fertility treatment that creates and discards excess embryos. . . .

The Personhood of an Embryo

There are two main arguments against permitting embryonic stem cell research. One holds that, despite its worthy ends, stem cell research is wrong because it involves the destruction of human embryos; the other worries that even if research on embryos is not wrong in itself, it would open the way to a slippery slope of dehumanizing practices, such as embryo farms, cloned babies, the use of fetuses for spare parts, and the commodification of human life.

The slippery slope objection is a practical one that deserves to be taken seriously. But its worries could be addressed by adopting regulatory safeguards to prevent embryo research from devolving into nightmare scenarios of exploitation and abuse. The first objection, however, is more philosophically challenging. Whether it is decisive depends on whether its view of the moral status of the embryo is correct.

Using cloned embryos for research is thus morally less troubling than using natural ones.

It is important to be clear, first of all, about the embryo from which stem cells are extracted. It is not a fetus. It has no recognizable human features or form. It is not an embryo implanted and growing in a woman's uterus. It is, rather, a blastocyst, a cluster of 180 to 200 cells, growing in a petri dish, barely visible to the naked eye. The blastocyst represents such an early stage of embryonic development that the cells it contains have not yet differentiated, or taken on the properties of particular organs or tissues—kidneys, muscles, spinal cord, and so on. This is why the stem cells that are extracted from the blastocyst hold the promise of developing, with proper coaxing in the lab, into any kind of cell the researcher wants to study or repair. The moral and political controversy arises from the fact that extracting the stem cells destroys the blastocyst.

To assess this controversy, one must begin by grasping the full force of the claim that the embryo is morally equivalent to a person, a fully developed human being. For those who hold this view, extracting stem cells from a blastocyst is as morally abhorrent as harvesting organs from a baby to save other people's lives. Some base this claim on the religious belief that ensoulment occurs at conception. . . .

The argument for the equal-moral-status view begins with the observations that every person was once an embryo, and that there is no nonarbitrary line between conception and adulthood that can tell us when personhood begins. It then asserts that, given the lack of such a line, we should regard the blastocyst as a person, morally equivalent to a fully developed human being. But this argument is not persuasive, for several reasons.

First, a small but not inconsequential point: While it is true that every one of us was once an embryo, none of us was ever a cloned blastocyst. So even if the fact of our embryonic origin did prove that embryos are persons, it would only condemn stem cell research on embryos produced by the union of egg and sperm, not stem cell research on cloned embryos. In fact, some participants in the stem cell debate have argued that cloned blastocysts are not, strictly speaking, embryos but biologic artifacts ("clonotes" rather than zygotes) that lack the moral status of naturally conceived human embryos. They argue that using cloned embryos for research is thus morally less troubling than using natural ones.

Second, even setting aside the question of the "clonote," the fact that every person began life as an embryo does not prove that embryos are persons. Consider an analogy: Although every oak tree was once an acorn, it does not follow that acorns are oak trees, or that I should treat the loss of an acorn eaten by a squirrel in my front yard as the same kind of loss as the death of an oak tree felled by a storm. Despite their developmental continuity, acorns and oak trees differ. So do human embryos and human beings, and in the same way. Just as acorns are potential oaks, human embryos are potential human beings. The distinction between actual persons and potential ones is not without ethical significance. Sentient creatures make claims on us that nonsentient ones do not; beings capable of experience and consciousness make higher claims still. Human life develops by degrees. . . .

Therapeutic Cloning Is a Noble Pursuit

We would do better to cultivate a more expansive appreciation of life as a gift that commands our reverence and restricts our use. Genetic engineering to create designer babies is the ultimate expression of the hubris that marks the loss of reverence for life as a gift. But stem cell research to cure debilitating disease, using unimplanted blastocysts, is a noble exercise of our human ingenuity to promote healing and to play our part in repairing the given world.

Those who warn of slippery slopes, embryo farms, and the commodification of ova and zygotes are right to worry but wrong to assume that embryo research necessarily opens us to these dangers. Rather than ban embryonic stem cell research and research cloning, we should allow them to proceed subject to regulations that embody the moral restraint appropriate to the mystery of the first stirrings of human life. Such regulations should include a ban on human reproductive cloning, reasonable limits on the length of time an embryo can be grown in the lab, licensing requirements for fertility clinics, restrictions on the commodification of eggs and sperm, and a stem cell bank to prevent proprietary interests from monopolizing access to stem cell lines. This approach, it seems to me, offers the best hope of avoiding the wanton use of nascent human life and making biomedical advance a blessing for health rather than an episode in the erosion of our human sensibilities.

10

Embryonic Stem Cell Research Threatens Women's Health

Diane Beeson and Abby Lippman

Diane Beeson has served as a consultant on projects related to genetic testing for numerous organizations, including the National Society of Genetic Counselors, National Institutes of Health, and the US Department of Energy. She has served on peer review committees for the National Human Genome Research Institute and has authored numerous articles in professional journals and anthologies. Abby Lippman, president of the Canadian Women's Health Network, is particularly interested in the politics of women's health. Her research has centered mainly on women's health and includes feminist studies of applied genetic and reproductive technologies as well as critical analyses of health and pharmaceutical policies.

In the pursuit of scientific and medical breakthroughs, scientists are in desperate need of multiple eggs from young women donors to be used for embryonic stem cell research. The harvesting of these eggs, however, involves the administration of hormonal drugs—drugs that have not been approved for such a purpose nor been adequately studied to assess their short- and long-term effects on women's health. Already evidence exists that egg donors have suffered from ovarian hyperstimulation syndrome (OHSS), with symptoms including nausea, abdominal distention, respiratory difficulty, renal failure, and ovarian rupture. Clearly there is cause to be concerned about the expanding demand for human eggs with its associated serious risks to young women's health.

Diane Beeson and Abby Lippman, "Egg Harvesting for Stem Cell Research: Medical Risks and Ethical Problems," *Reproductive BioMedicine Online*, August 14, 2006. Reproduced by permission of Elsevier B.V.

Women's health and human rights advocates throughout the world are increasingly concerned that overzealous pursuit of new scientific discoveries may once again be threatening women's health. This time, young women are being asked to donate or sell their ova, not only for use in fertility clinics, but increasingly for non-clinical use in experimental cloning research. The harvesting of multiple eggs often involves the administration of hormonal drugs that have not been approved for this purpose. These drugs also have not been adequately studied for their long-term effects on women despite research providing some evidence of significant harm to women in both the short and long term. The collection of eggs for embryo cloning research is being conducted in the context of an international race for dominance in—and commercialization of—the production of embryonic stem cells and related products that may result in substantial private financial gain while offering no therapeutic benefits that are accessible to the vast majority. While much speculation about its ultimate clinical value and potential benefits is fuelling this embryo cloning research, the risks of egg harvesting, both short and long term, do not receive adequate attention. In this article, we focus on some of the major concerns: a research climate marked by conflicts of interest; the misleading use of language to describe research goals; and a commercial push that may lead to the exploitation of young women. These are leading to the formation of an international coalition of critics who seek to curb a trend to the use of women as sources of raw materials for research, experimentation, and product development related to stem cell research.

Short-Term Effects

Since the birth of the world's first 'test-tube baby,' Louise Brown, in 1978, egg-harvesting procedures have become increasingly widely used in IVF [in vitro fertilization]. This has led to the assumption by many that egg collection practices have been proven to be safe. Unfortunately this is not the case. In North America, at least, most of these procedures have been conducted in private fertility clinics without independent oversight and, until recently, without systematic voluntary reporting even of serious side effects. The existing research is very limited and often retrospective. Despite a serious absence of long-term independent assessments of the effects of egg harvesting on women's health, this research already reveals a multitude of problems resulting from these procedures. However, in spite of occasional calls for caution and warnings that exposing healthy women to these risks is 'morally and ethically unacceptable' little action is being taken to alert potential egg providers to the dangers of egg harvesting.

The absence of adequate follow-up means that the long-term risks of ovarian stimulation are poorly understood.

The harvesting of multiple eggs is an invasive and uncomfortable two-stage process requiring many clinic visits, multiple injections of hormones, and minor surgery at the least. Both stages, ovarian suppression and what is known as 'ovarian stimulation', require the use of powerful hormones and other drugs to manipulate a woman's body into producing many, often a dozen or more, eggs at a time rather than the normal one or two. The mature eggs are then collected surgically for use in IVF or in research.

The most immediate serious risk from ovarian stimulation is ovarian hyperstimulation syndrome (OHSS). The American Society of Reproductive Medicine (ASRM) acknowledges that mild forms of OHSS occur in 10–20% of cycles, and others have published similar estimates. Symptoms of mild forms of OHSS include nausea, vomiting, diarrhea, and abdominal distention. These symptoms may persist or worsen over time to include rapid weight gain, accumulation of serous fluid in the spaces between tissues and organs in the pleural and abdominal cavity, respiratory difficulty, and other abnormalities. More severe forms of OHSS requiring hospitalization and 'by no means rare' according to the ASRM. Thromboembolism, renal failure, adult respiratory distress, and haemorrhage from ovarian rupture have all been reported, but the rates of occurrence vary widely. As of June 2005 five women in the UK [United Kingdom] were known to have died of OHSS.

Long-Term Effects

The absence of adequate follow-up means that the long-term risks of ovarian stimulation are poorly understood. As Suzanne Parisian former Chief Medical Officer of the United States Food and Drug Administration (FDA), explains, 'Pharmaceutical firms have not been required by either the government or physicians to collect safety data for IVF drugs regarding risk of cancer or other serious health conditions despite the drugs having been available in the United States for several decades.' One drug commonly used in the first phase of egg harvesting, Lupron (leuprolide acetate), has not been approved for this purpose, but rather is used 'off label.' Another drug, Antagon, has been approved for such use, but no data are available on its long-term safety. The US FDA currently has on file more than 6000 complaints regarding Lupron, including 25 reported deaths, but none of this has been investigated or analysed sufficiently to provide women contemplating egg donation the information necessary for making an informed choice. . . .

Beyond direct risks to the women undergoing ovarian stimulation, one must also consider possible effects of exposure to the drugs used on the offspring of treated women. Here, too, human data are sorely lacking. However, a recent report that ovarian stimulation treatment in mice results in several significant abnormalities in their offspring does provide reason for concern. These effects include growth retardation, a delay in ossification (bone development) and an eightfold increase in a significant rib deformity. Questions about the degree to which these findings have implications for the use of ovarian stimulation treatments in women should be answered before thousands of women are exposed to ovarian stimulation purely for research purposes. As the example of the hormone diethyistilbestrol (DES) described below illustrates, risks to offspring from exposure to hormones used in ovarian stimulation would not be the first instance of ill effects of hormones being carried into future generations.

Widespread exposure of healthy women to incompletely-assessed drug interventions can be dangerous.

The risks of egg harvesting, like those of any medical intervention, must always be weighed against potential benefits. A woman who undergoes ovarian stimulation in an attempt to become pregnant or to provide eggs for another woman faces virtually the same risks as one who is exposed solely to obtain her eggs for research. (The amount and manner in which the drugs are administered could change the degree of risk.) But the risk-benefit calculus is very different for each of these women. One has a 10–40% chance of producing a baby either for herself or another women, while the other is but a subject in a research project with still uncertain benefits. Calls for more systematic long-term follow-up are in the interest of women in both categories—as are demands that both categories be informed sufficiently to meet the consent criteria for clinical or research projects.

Given the multiple unknowns regarding the long-term consequences of ovarian stimulation, it is appropriate to place today's practices in historical context. The exposure of large numbers of women to heavy doses of exogenous hormones of unknown safety or effectiveness is not new. An early example dates from 1947 regarding widespread prescribing of DES to pregnant women to prevent miscarriage or premature birth.

Even though DES was shown not to prevent miscarriage as early as 1953, its use continued for almost 20 years, until landmark 1971 study documented the alarming occurrence of an often fatal form of vaginal cancer in the young daughters born to women who had been given DES. Five to ten million women worldwide were exposed to DES before its dangers were well understood. The full extent of the damage, which ironically includes infertility in female offspring and problems for many DES sons as well and which may be continuing into a third generation, may never be known although some longitudinal research into those who were exposed *in utero* and their offspring is ongoing.

More recently, hormone replacement therapy (HRT), after being vigorously marketed to menopausal women for decades, often advertised as a way of preventing future disease, was found to increase risks for a variety of serious health problems and to contribute little to preventing others. Two randomized clinical trials, one of oestrogen alone, and one of oestrogen plus progesterone, had to be stopped because of clear evidence of serious adverse effects. Certainly we must learn from experience with DES and HRT that early reassuring studies often prove wrong in the longer term, and that widespread exposure of healthy women to incompletely-assessed drug interventions can be dangerous. Policy makers have a particular obligation to protect non-patient 'donors' from the possible threat of irreversible harm by insisting that prevention takes precedence over everything else. . . .

Conflicts of Interest and Misleading Language

An array of powerful social and economic pressures encourages researchers and research advocates to overlook or play down risks to egg providers. For example, some physicians who harvest eggs are also involved in stem cell research. Seeking consent from women in these circumstances is problematic when clinicians have an interest in obtaining their eggs.

This conflict exists whether or not the eggs are being extracted from a woman who is undergoing the procedures for the purpose of IVF, and threatens to violate the requirement in the Declaration of Geneva (1948) of the World Medical Association that physicians give '[T]he health of my patient . . . first consideration.' It also contravenes the International Code of Medical Ethics that deems unethical any intervention that 'could weaken physical or mental resistance of a human being' unless used in her interest. When the clinician and researcher are the same person, as is often the case, women are left vulnerable to pressures to provide eggs—especially when payment of any kind is offered. . . .

Critiques of egg-harvesting procedures by women's health advocates and feminists have raised further concerns about how the apparently purposeful use of misleading language to describe this research has the potential to be coercive. Engaging with embryo stem cell research requires that laypersons understand complex scientific issues, but this task has been made unnecessarily difficult by the language often used by scientists trying to garner public support for cloning research and, in the US, votes for funding or for egg 'donation'.

Too often, for example, the focus is put on promises of imminent 'cures' for diseases, and help for one or more of the conditions many of our family members may already have and which most of us will one day develop, a stance that even a vocal advocate of stem cell research has characterized as bordering on 'over-promising at best and delusional fantasising at worst.'

Moreover, kept from the public discourse is the scientifically accurate term for the outcome or end result: a 'clone' or 'clonal embryo'. Instead, in promoting their research agendas, proponents of cloning research talk of somatic cell nuclear transfer (SCNT), a process. This practice tends to obscure the purpose of the process, which is to create a human embryo comprising cells that are genetically identical to those of an existing human being. Also left out of the discourse is the fact that embryo cloning is the 'gateway' technology to other non-therapeutic goals fervently espoused by certain prominent individuals such as former Nobel laureate James Watson. These goals include the genetic modification of offspring to influence such traits as intelligence, height, and other characteriztics, and in ways that would inevitably affect future generations, for better or worse.

Although most who support research cloning condemn reproductive cloning—and thus endorse proposals to ban any implantation of a clonal embryo into a woman—many countries such as the United States do not yet have a universal ban on human reproductive cloning. This fact makes it possible for any advances in this research to be applied to human reproductive cloning regardless of the intent of researchers.

There has been very little exploration of the emotional impact of selling one's eggs.

Many discussions of this topic also tend to use the inaccurate term 'therapeutic' cloning—rather than 'research' cloning—and thus further cloud the reality of what is now possible. Many potential research participants, as well as the broader public, now wrongly believe that therapies are likely to result in the near future and thus see providing eggs as a way to held others.

The combination of ambiguous language, financial pressures to push the research, and promises of imminent 'cures' clearly shape the decision-making context of potential providers of eggs for research. . . .

Violations of the Doctor-Patient Relationship and the Emotional Impact on Egg Donors

Eggs must be harvested by doctors, but egg collection for research purposes marks a transformation in the doctor-patient relationship, which has historically been based on the assumption that the doctor's primary goal and responsibility is to protect or restore the patient's health. When the doctor becomes the agent of a third party, in this case a researcher, and relates to the patient with the researcher's interests in mind, the doctor is violating the basic assumptions of the doctor-patient relationship. Abandonment of these traditional assumptions leaves the patient in a particularly vulnerable position. Physicians also deserve to be spared the distortions this creates in their relationship with their patients. It is the appropriate role of policy makers and physicians to see that patients, who often feel a need to please their health providers by being 'good patients' to get the best possible care, are not called upon to make decisions that are based on an oversimplified understanding of information on which even experts are not in full agreement. Such situations would be in violation of the traditional understandings of the role of medical expertise in the doctor-patient relationship.

When traditional assumptions about the physician-patient relationships are violated, as they can be when eggs are being taken to serve the interests of the physician or another third party, not a loved one, it is not surprising that some women will find the experience emotionally damaging. Yet, there has been very little exploration of the emotional impact of selling one's eggs. A small qualitative US study of 33 paid US 'donors' reported that at least seven 'felt that promises clinic staff made when they were trying to recruit the women were not kept once the women were engaged in the process'. These ranged from requests for a specific kind of anaesthesia or for a female physician to the promise of follow-up care. The authors report that many of the women described their care as cold and impersonal: They used metaphors such as 'farm animals', 'produce', 'meat', and 'prostitution' to describe how the experience made them feel. This suggests we need to examine the impact of egg harvesting on the emotional well being of egg providers and also the social fabric before expanding these practices.

Clearly there is cause to be concerned about the negative short and long-term effects of the expanding demand for human eggs on young women's health, and possibly for their offspring as well. Risks that may be justifiable for women seeking to become pregnant are not justifiable for the purposes of research. Encouraging young healthy women to risk damage to their own health by providing eggs for hypothetical treatments for others is not ethically or socially justifiable.

11

The Government Should Establish Egg Donor Registries

Jennifer Schneider

Jennifer Schneider is a physician, writer, and lecturer. She is the author of nine books and numerous articles in professional journals, has served as an expert witness in legal settings, and has appeared as a media guest on television and radio.

For medical researchers and fertility clinics, egg donation has become serious business; the more eggs, the better and more profitable the business. As a result, young women are pursued with offers of as much as $100,000 to donate their eggs, but are not given accurate information regarding the health risks involved. In fact, not much information about the health risks—such as hormone-related cancers—is actually known because few long-term follow-up studies have been undertaken. To protect young women, the government must create a comprehensive egg donor registry so that proper oversight is met and long-term health effects can be determined.

I'm a physician. I'm also the mother of a young woman [Jessica] who, like thousands of other college students at elite universities, decided to supplement her income by donating her eggs for money. And like all other egg donors, she did it without understanding that the long-term risks of this procedure are unknown. She underwent the procedure three times,

Jennifer Schneider, "The Politics of Women's Health: Egg Donation for IVF and Stem Cell Research," Testimony at the Congressional Briefing on Human Egg Trafficking, November 14, 2007, *Our Bodies, Ourselves*, www.ourbodiesourselves.org. Reproduced with permission of Jennifer Schneider.

and then went on with her life. Six years later she was dead of a disease that usually affects people my age, not hers—colon cancer. She had no family history of this disease, and genetic studies of her tissue subsequently showed that she was not at genetic risk of colon cancer.

Since her death I've researched what is known about the long-term risks of colon cancer in egg donors, and I'm here to tell you that hardly anything is known, because once a young woman walks out of an IVF [in vitro fertilization] clinic, she is of no interest to anyone. No one keeps track of her health. In fact, the people who benefit from egg donations—IVF clinics and researchers—have every reason to avoid follow-up of egg donors and studies of their possible long-term risks. (After Jessica's death I learned the name of her egg broker and phoned her. I told her Jessica had died of a potentially genetic disease and the broker needed to tell the recipients of Jessica's eggs about this, because their child/children will need to be tested. The broker told me that she only keeps records for a few years, and had already destroyed all records pertaining to Jessica, so that the broker no longer had information about the recipients. Very convenient!)

The IVF clinics make enormous sums of money from egg donation, and the researchers want to maximize the number of eggs they have. That's why, as in Great Britain, we need government intervention. I'm here to tell you why I think it is very important for Congress to mandate egg donor registries and keep track of egg donors.

A Personal Story of an Egg Donor

Jessica fits the classic description of an ideal egg donor: beautiful (she modeled in her teens), bright (Stanford graduate), tall (6 feet tall), athletic, talented, artistic. A short film she made at college won the first prize for best short film that year at the San Francisco Film Festival. She composed songs, played piano and guitar, and was lead singer in a rock band at college. Later she composed more classical musicals.

When Jessica phoned me to tell me she was considering being an egg donor, I said, "My main concern is your safety. Is this safe?" She said, "They told me there are some risks associated with the procedure, such as bleeding or infection, and that's about it." She said, "I'm having this done at a very respected IVF clinic. I'm sure they'll take good care of me." Even though I'm a highly trained medical professional, I assumed that what she was telling me was the facts. The first time she donated her eggs, a pregnancy resulted. This made her a "proven donor," an even more desirable category. A couple of months later, the egg broker phoned her to say another couple wanted to use her, and was willing to pay twice as much. She did 3 egg cycles in all.

Jessica then entered a graduate school program in film making, and was finishing up her master's degree when she developed abdominal pain. A work-up showed advanced colon cancer, very unusual in a 29-year-old. I knew that average survival with the best treatments available was 18 months. Jessica had to drop out of school. She underwent chemotherapy, massive surgery, and radiation when she developed metastases in her bones and then her brain. She then developed metastases in her lungs and gradually lost her ability to breathe. She died at age 31.

Long-term risks of egg donation are unknown.

During her almost 2 years of fighting her cancer, she composed a musical based on the story of "Hansel and Gretel." Her theater company planned to mount a production of this musical, and Jessica's greatest wish was to see it performed. She brought her computer with her to chemotherapy sessions and hospitalizations, and continued composing while lying in bed. But she died 3 weeks before her musical premiered at the

New York International Fringe Festival, where it won a prize for Best Music for that year, 2003. The *New York Times* Arts section had a lead article about Jessica and her musical. It was titled, "Premiere Draws A Crowd, and Tears, For Absent Composer." The *NBC Today* show ran a piece about Jessica.

A Closer Look

Her death was unexplained. When she was first diagnosed, the first thing she—and I—thought of was could it have been the large doses of hormones she received for the egg retrieval. Jessica asked her oncologist, who told her that there was no evidence supporting a role of ovarian hyperstimulation in causing colon cancer.

But last year [2006] I ran across an article by Dr. Kamal Ahuja, a specialist in in vitro fertilization (IVF), that described a young woman who donated eggs for her infertile sister, and a few years later was diagnosed with advanced colon cancer and died. This got me thinking seriously about the possible role of ovarian stimulation in causing her colon cancer. I began doing a lot of reading, and communicating with specialists in the field. What I learned was very disturbing. Here is what I learned:

- Egg donors are commodities.

- Long-term risks of egg donation are unknown.

- IVF clinics and researchers have a serious conflict of interest.

- The government needs to intervene.

The first baby born by in vitro fertilization (IVF) was born in 1978. The first IVF baby using a donated egg was born in 1984. In 1992 there were about 1800 egg donor cycles. In 2004 there were 15,175 egg donor cycles. This exponential increase is escalating further now because of the new huge demand for eggs for stem cell research.

[A] front-page article in *Arizona Daily News* on Nov 4, 2007 (originally published in the *Minneapolis Star Tribune*) was titled "New Life for Sale: Human eggs focus of booming $3B industry." Quotes [from the article]:

> Caitlin K. sees it as a classic case of supply and demand. After all, one of her eggs goes to waste every month, so she might as well share it with a woman who can use it. She thinks the $8,000 she can get is a reasonable price for helping someone create a life . . . Caitlin K, 24, is a bit player in a $3 billion business that is thriving on the Internet . . . But as it flourished, some are warning that the freewheeling marketplace is turning the creation of human life into a commercial enterprise that cries out for consumer protection. Nowhere is this more evident than in the exploding market for human eggs, where there are few laws protecting the rights and health of donors and parents. . . .

> Donors are becoming more savvy. . . . Girls are doing it because it helps with their finances. . . Would-be parents pay the fee to the egg donor themselves, in addition to the $15,000 or more than goes to the agency for insurance, and the donor's medical and legal costs.

The egg broker also profits with a hefty fee. And the medical insurance purchased for the egg donor undoubtedly does not cover late medical costs, such as was the case with Jessica's illness.

- Egg donors are not followed up.

- They don't have their own doctors.

- The known short-term risks (ovarian hyperstimulation syndrome) are underplayed (no one told Jessica anything about this, yet young women have died).

- Long-term risks are not known.

- Egg donors sign consent forms without knowing the risks, because the risks are not known.

- Once they leave the IVF clinic they are of no interest to anyone.

Downplaying the Risks

The above article mentions a website called Egg Donation Inc. so I visited it. Its motto is "Where Dreams Come True." It claims to be the oldest and largest donor website in the world, with a stable of over 1,000 available egg donors. This detailed website discusses medical, legal, and psychological issues. Its emphasis is on altruism, although the reality is that the main motivator for egg donors is money. It provides testimonials from 2 egg donors. One says, in part, "Ever since my teens I've wanted to do something that will make a difference in someone else's life." The other says, in part, "The opportunity to help someone else without wanting something back really only comes around a few times in life." The website says nothing about risks, other than in the legal section which states "medical professionals will discuss risks."

The quick money overwhelms any real attention to potential risks.

Yesterday I googled "egg donation" and got 487,000 hits. Many offer payment for egg donors. Some list extremely specific characteristics they seek—particular ethnic types, religion, eye color, type of education and interests, etc.—and offer sums as high as $100,000 for the right donor.

Young women are lured by these offers. The risks are minimized. Additionally, the young women are unlikely to understand the huge difference between the statements "There are no known long-term risks," and "There are no long-term risks." Moreover, the quick money overwhelms any real attention to potential risks. Potential egg donors need their own doctor, they need an impartial person who can counsel them and who is not a part of the egg donor industry. Instead they are perceived as commodities rather than as individual human beings of value. Instead, they are counseled by employees of the egg broker and the IVF clinic, who naturally want as many women as possible to sell their eggs.

IVF clinics and researchers are interested in getting as many eggs as possible, which involves high doses of hormones.

There have been no long term studies of egg donors. There is a real need for such studies. But they will not happen until there is a mandatory egg donor registry so that there is contact information for egg donors so they can be followed up for years.

Here's what we know so far about the relationship between hormonal stimulation and cancer:

1. [There have been] studies of infertile woman who have had ovarian stimulation in order to harvest their own eggs. (They are not comparable to young egg donors— older; infertility itself is associated with increased risk of some cancers; if they get pregnant subsequently, the hormonal milieu of pregnancy may mitigate some of the effects of ovarian stimulation.) A study of over 12,000 such infertile women was published in 2005 (Altuis et al). It found a 1.8-fold increase in the risk of uterine cancer following ovarian stimulation. The study didn't follow enough women for a long enough time, but it did find that the greater the number of years since donation, the greater the risk of breast cancer.

2. [There have been] studies of effects of female hormones in general. It is known that treatment with estrogen causes an increase in the risk of estrogen-related cancers such as breast and ovarian cancer. In the past few years, now that fewer women take hormones after menopause,

there has been a decline in breast cancer. Women who have a uterus and take estrogen are at increased risk of uterine cancer, which is why they are also advised to take a progesterone, which counteracts the increased risk.

Why are private agencies not interested in the well-being of egg donors? Because they have a lot to gain from encouraging egg donors—money from desperate infertile couples, and eggs for research. IVF clinics are highly lucrative. They are the "cash cows" of university Ob-gyn departments. Researchers want as many eggs as possible.

A Conflict of Interest

There is now research taking place on "natural" IVF. Women don't need to be given high doses of hormones in order to produce a single egg—they do it once a month on their own. It's possible for IVF clinics to obtain a single egg from an egg donor without stimulating her ovaries, and it's clearly safer. But it's also a lot less efficient—several months of ultrasounds and egg retrieval may be necessary for a pregnancy, and certainly researchers will get fewer eggs for research. So IVF clinics and researchers are interested in getting as many eggs as possible, which involves high doses of hormones.

There is urgent need for proper oversight and medical care of egg donors.

In 2006 the American Society of Reproductive Medicine's [ASRM] Ethics Committee published guidelines on payments to egg donors. They suggested a "reasonable" fee of $5,000, and a maximum of $10,000. But they did not put in place any way of enforcing these guidelines, which are widely ignored. The members of ASRM are primarily physicians working in IVF clinics, the same clinics who want to attract as many donors as possible, by offering them increasingly large fees.

Private agencies and researchers can't be expected to police themselves. This reality has been recognized in other countries. Great Britain, Canada, and Israel all have outlawed the sale of eggs. Eggs are similar to other organs, and the sale of organs is outlawed in the U.S. The sale of organs is outlawed because otherwise the financial incentives may outweigh consideration of the donor's best interest. The U.S., on the other hand, seems to consider egg donation in the same category as sperm donation rather than subject to existing laws regarding organ donation. Clearly, sperm donation does not involve risks, unlike egg donation.

There is urgent need for proper oversight and medical care of egg donors. There are two patients—the infertile woman and the egg donor, it's time that the egg donor cease to be the forgotten member of the team. This country needs a comprehensive egg donor registry, which will enable research on the long-term effects of egg donation.

Organizations to Contact

The editors have compiled the following list of organizations concerned with the issues debated in this book. The descriptions are derived from materials provided by the organizations. All have publications or information available for interested readers. The list was compiled on the date of publication of the present volume; street and online addresses may change. Be aware that many organizations take several weeks or longer to respond to inquiries, so allow as much time as possible.

American Association for the Advancement of Science (AAAS)

1200 New York Ave. NW, Washington, DC 20005
(202) 326-6400
e-mail: webmaster@aaas.org
website: www.aaas.org

Established in 1848, the AAAS is an international organization with the goal of advancing scientific inquiry worldwide. The AAAS provides a forum for educators, students, and the general public to learn more about the possibilities of emerging sciences. On the topic of embryonic experimentation, the AAAS promotes ethical research practices with hopes that those suffering from debilitating diseases will benefit from the findings. Among the organization's publications are the global weekly journal *Science* and *Science Translational Medicine: Integrating Medicine and Science.* Its website EurekAlert.org provides breaking science news from around the globe.

American Life League (ALL)

P.O. Box 1350, Stafford, VA 22555
(540) 659-4171 • fax: (540) 659-2586
e-mail: info@all.org
website: www.all.org

The American Life League is a pro-life organization dedicated to promoting ideals and government policies that preserve the sanctity of all human life. The group is openly and adamantly opposed to abortion, embryonic stem cell research, and birth control. ALL publishes news releases, commentaries, *Judie's Blog*, and sponsors numerous organizations and events that aid in educating the public about pro-life practices.

Bedford Stem Cell Research Foundation (BSCRF)

P.O. Box 1028, Bedford, MA   01730
(617) 281-7902 • fax: (617) 623-9447
e-mail: info@bedfordresearch.org
website: www.bedfordresearch.org

The BSCRF is an independent, non-federally funded, non-profit biomedical institute that conducts stem cell related research for diseases presently considered incurable. The foundation established an ethics advisory board that supervises its human egg donor program. BSCRF publishes *Science Highlights*, which contains monthly articles written by Ann A. Kiessling, PhD, and *Foundation News*, which describes the latest news events regarding biomedical research.

Center for Bioethics and Human Dignity (CBHD)

2065 Half Day Rd., Deerfield, IL   60015
(847) 317-8180 • fax: (847) 317-8101
e-mail: info@cbhd.org
website: www.cbhd.org

The CBHD investigates ethical issues of emerging biotechnology from a Christian perspective, and in 2009 launched the Global Bioethics Education Initiative (GBEI) to further advance Christian bioethics. The center publishes position statements and overviews on many issues including cloning, reproductive ethics, and stem cell research. In its position statement on stem cell research, the center provides ethical, legal, and scientific objections to the practices of embryonic stem cell research that kill the embryo in order to harvest stem cells. The CBHD sponsors many conferences each year concerning bioethics.

Center for Genetics and Society (CGS)

1936 University Ave., Suite 350, Berkeley, CA   94704
(510) 625-0819 • fax: (510) 665-8760
e-mail: info@geneticsandsociety.org
website: www.geneticsandsociety.org

The Center for Genetics and Society is a nonprofit information and public affairs organization working to encourage responsible uses and effective governance of human genetic and
reproductive technologies. Among the organization's publications are the newsletter *Weekly News & Views*, the 2009 report
"Next Steps for Stem Cell Research and Related Policies," the
Fact Sheet "Human Embryonic Stem Cell Research: Frequently
Asked Questions and Fact Sheet," and the *Biopolitical Times*
blog.

Coalition for the Advancement of Medical Research (CAMR)

2021 K St. NW, Suite 305, Washington, DC   20006
(202) 725-0339
e-mail: CAMResearch@yahoo.com
website: www.camradvocacy.org

The Coalition for the Advancement of Medical Research is a
coalition of organizations that support continued research of
embryonic stem cells. Members of CAMR include patient
groups, universities, and scientific societies. The coalition's
website provides extensive information on the curative potential of embryonic stem cells and the need for increased funding, and in 2009 CAMR published the white paper *A Catalyst
for Cures: Embryonic Stem Cell Research*.

Do No Harm: The Coalition of Americans for Research Ethics

1100 H St. NW, Suite 700, Washington, DC   20005
(202) 347-6840 • fax: (202) 347-6849
website: www.stemcellresearch.org

Do No Harm is an organization that promotes medical research and treatment that does not result in the destruction of
human life or human embryos. The organization promotes

adult stem cell research as a viable alternative to embryonic stem cell research. The group has published numerous fact sheets, and its website contains links to news and commentary on stem cell research.

The Hastings Center
21 Malcolm Gordon Rd., Garrison, NY   10524
(845) 424-4040
e-mail: mail@thehastingscenter.org
website: www.thehastingscenter.org

The Hastings Center is a nonprofit organization that examines the ethical issues surrounding current biotechnological advancements. Its interdisciplinary teams present a range of viewpoints on select topics. The center publishes two bimonthly journals concerning bioethics, *The Hastings Center Report* and *IRB: Ethics and Human Research*, as well as special reports and the *Bioethics Forum* blog.

International Society for Stem Cell Research (ISSCR)
111 Deerlake Rd., Suite 100, Deerfield, IL   60005
(847) 509-1944 • fax: (847) 480-9282
e-mail: isscr@isscr.org
website: www.isscr.org

In promoting the advancement of stem cell research, the independent, nonprofit ISSCR seeks to accurately inform the public about the possibilities and goals of this research. The society encourages ethical embryonic research in hopes that its findings will yield treatment for many, otherwise incurable diseases. The ISSCR has openly opposed and lobbied against US and UN bans on embryonic stem cell research. Educational materials are available for the public on the organization's website, and it publishes position statements and the monthly newsletter *The Pulse*.

National Right to Life Committee (NRLC)
512 10th St. NW, Washington, DC   20004
(202) 626-8800

e-mail: nrlc@nrlc.org
website: www.nrlc.org

The NRLC was founded following the decision of the US Supreme Court case *Roe vs. Wade*, which federally legalized abortion. The organization acts as a lobbying group that promotes a pro-life government agenda, including advocating for a ban on nontherapeutic human embryo experimentation. The NRLC publishes the monthly *National Right to Life News* and the *National Right to Life Communications* blog.

The Presidential Commission for the Study of Bioethical Issues

1425 New York Ave. NW, Suite C-100, Washington, DC   2006
(202) 233-3960 • fax: (202) 233-3990
e-mail: info@bioethics.gov
website: www.bioethics.gov

President Barack Obama established the Presidential Commission for the study of Bioethical Issues within the Department of Health and Human Services in November 2009. The commission's goal is to identify and promote policies and practices that ensure scientific research, healthcare delivery, and technological innovation are conducted in an ethical and responsible manner. The commission maintains a blog and publishes news items, reports, and transcripts from meetings and sessions on its website.

Society for Developmental Biology (SDB)

9650 Rockville Pike, Bethesda, MD   20814
(301) 634-7815 • fax: (301) 634-7825
e-mail: sdb@sdbonline.org
website: www.sdbonline.org

SDB is a global organization that was founded in 1939 with the mission of promoting increased research and education in the field of developmental biology. Members of the SDB have supported a voluntary moratorium on human cloning. Regarding the issue of therapeutic cloning, the SDB Board of

Trustees believes only limited knowledge can be gained by researching only existing stem cell lines, and it supports the creation of a new oversight committee to address bioethical concerns in the United States. The society publishes the journal *Developmental Biology.*

Westchester Institute for Ethics & the Human Person
P.O. Box 78, Thornwood, NY   10594
e-mail: info@westchesterinstitute.net
website: www.westchesterinstitute.net

The Westchester Institute is a research institute centered on the classic Catholic moral view. The institute studies such contemporary issues as the moral status of the human embryo, morally feasible alternatives to embryo-based biomedical research, and the relationship between religion and science in modern society. On its website, the institute publishes *In Focus*, which features articles of interest and the *White Paper Series*, including "When Does Human Life Begin? A Scientific Perspective."

Bibliography

Books

Michael Bellomo   *The Stem Cell Divide: The Facts, the Fiction, and the Fear Driving the Greatest Scientific, Political, and Religious Debate of Our Time.* New York: AMACOM, 2006.

Thomas F. Budinger and Miriam D. Budinger   *Ethics of Emerging Technologies: Scientific Facts and Moral Challenges.* Hoboken, NJ: John Wiley & Sons, 2006.

Bruce M. Carlson   *Stem Cell Anthology: Stem Cell Biology, Tissue Engineering, Cloning, Regenerative Medicine, and Biology.* Burlington, MA: Academic Press, 2009.

Cynthia Fox   *Cell of Cells: The Global Race to Capture and Control the Stem Cell.* New York: W.W. Norton & Company, 2007.

Herbert Gottweis, Brian Salter, and Catherine Waldby   *The Global Politics of Human Embryonic Stem Cell Science.* New York: Palgrave Macmillan, 2009.

Louis M. Guenin   *The Morality of Embryo Use.* New York: Cambridge University Press, 2008.

Eve Herold   *Stem Cell Wars: Inside Stories from the Frontlines.* New York: Palgrave Macmillan, 2006.

Scott Klusendorf   *The Case for Life: Equipping Christians to Engage the Culture.* Wheaton, IL: Crossway Books, 2009.

Ronald A. Lindsay   *Future Bioethics: Overcoming Taboos, Myths, and Dogmas.* Amherst, NY: Prometheus Books, 2008.

Kristen Renwick Monroe, Ronald Miller, and Jerome Tobis   *Fundamentals of the Stem Cell Debate: The Scientific, Religious, Ethical, and Political Issues.* Berkeley, CA: University of California Press, 2008.

Ted Peters   *Sacred Cells?: Why Christians Should Support Stem Cell Research.* Lanham, MD: Rowman & Littlefield, 2008.

Ted Peters   *The Stem Cell Debate.* Minneapolis, MN: Fortress Press, 2007.

Christopher Thomas Scott   *Stem Cell Now: A Brief Introduction to the Coming Medical Revolution.* New York: Plume, 2006.

Stephen Sullivan, Chad A. Cowan, and Kevin Eggan   *Human Embryonic Stem Cells: The Practical Handbook.* Hoboken, NJ: John Wiley & Sons, 2007.

Periodicals and Internet Sources

Paul Basken   "Scientists Are Optimistic as Appeals Court Lifts Injunction Against Stem-Cell Research," *The Chronicle of Higher Education*, September 9, 2010.

Fritz J. Baumgartner   "Federal Funding of Human Embryonic Stem Cell Research Revisited: Does the Nobility of Hoped-For Ends Absolve Us?" April 22, 2009. www.ctsnet.org.

Center for Genetics and Society   "Human Embryonic Stem Cell Research Frequently Asked Questions and Fact Sheet," January 9, 2009. www.geneticsandsociety.org.

Alayne Chappell   "Donating Eggs: The Potential Implications of an Unregulated Industry," *Golden Gate Xpress*, May 5, 2010.

Michael Collins   "Truth in Egg-Donor Advertising," *The Daily Princetonian*, November 21, 2008.

Jill Colvin   "The Baby Factory: One Young Woman Faces the Temptation of Selling Her Eggs," *New York Press*, September 5, 2007.

Peter Crosta   "What Are Stem Cells?" MedicalNewsToday.com, 2010.

Michael Fumento   "Embryonic Research Driven by Greed, Not Science," *New York Post*, July 15, 2009.

Bernadine Healy   "Why Embryonic Stem Cells Are Obsolete," *U.S. News & World Report*, March 4, 2009.

Mark Johnson   "Better Path to Embryonic Cell Production," *MCT News Service*, November 15, 2010.

Claudia Kalb   "A New Stem Cell Era," *Newsweek*, March 9, 2009.

Jeanne Lenzer   "Have We Entered the Stem Cell Era?" *Discover*, November 2009.

Yuval Levin   "Public Opinion and the Embryo Debates," *The New Atlantis*, Spring 2008.

Kim Lute   "I, and Others, Know Firsthand the Need to Study Stem Cells," *Atlanta Journal-Constitution*, April 10, 2009.

John O'Brien   "Stem-Cell Research Can Promote Life, Dignity and Discovery," *Orlando Sentinel*, June 13, 2008.

Alice Park   "New Rules Expand Federal Funding of Stem Cells," *Time*, July 7, 2009.

Alice Park   "Stem-Cell Research: The Quest Resumes," *Time*, January 29, 2009.

Roni Caryn Rabin   "As Demand for Donor Eggs Soars, High Prices Stir Ethical Concerns," *New York Times*, May 15, 2007.

Malcolm Ritter   "Adult Stem Cell Research Far Ahead of Embryonic," *Associated Press*, August 1, 2010.

Teisha Rowland   "Human Embryonic Stem Cells: A Decade of Discovery, Controversy, and Potential," AllThingsStem Cell.com, April 19, 2009.

Michael J. Sandel   "Embryo Ethics," *Boston Globe*, April 8, 2007.

Emily Singer   "Human Therapeutic Cloning at a Standstill," *Technology Review*, October 9, 2007.

Loane Skene   "Donating Eggs for Research Is Tough—So Why Not Pay For It?" TheAge.com, July 13, 2009.

Rob Stein   "Researchers Find Safer Way to Produce Stem Cell Alternative," *Washington Post*, March 2, 2009.

John Tierney   "Are Scientists Playing God? It Depends on Your Religion," *New York Times*, November 20, 2007.

Sarah Wildman   "Making Up for Lost Time on Stem Cells," *The Guardian*, March 10, 2009.

Index